1

"More Precious Than Rubies"

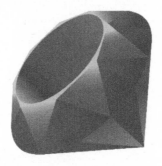

Daily Jewels of Inspiration

"More Precious Than Rubies"
DAILY JEWELS OF INSPIRATION
By John Weigelt

PREFACE

I chose the title of this book, "More Precious Than Rubies", in light of how the book of Proverbs, chapter 3, verses 13-15 describes wisdom and understanding – "more precious than rubies". After writing my first book, "24 Karat" Daily Nuggets of Inspiration, which I named for pure gold being 24-karat, I continued with my daily routine of reading one chapter from the book of Psalms and one chapter from Proverbs. I then focused on one or two verses, meditated on those verses, and then wrote a short message on how the verses inspired me. I continued to send out these messages daily to our church members, other pastors, and many friends. This book is another collection of 150 daily messages based on the books of Psalms and Proverbs. The intent of this book is to read one message a day, consider the short devotional message that follows, and then do your own meditation. I find the Bible to be a valuable resource for daily living and encouragement.

ACKNOWLEDGMENTS: I also want to give a heart-felt "Thank You" to Paul Herbert and Elander Hill for helping me edit this book. Their encouragement, suggestions, and advice are much appreciated.

My wife, Judy, and I have known Pastor John Weigelt for almost forty years. During these years, he has served as a confidante and counselor as well as being a true friend. John and his wife, Margaret, are gifted with the spirit of hospitality and it has been my privilege to be their guest many times during the years I have known them.

John is blessed with a generous heart and an excellent spirit. He has always had a heart to help and encourage others, whether behind the pulpit or ministering one on one to the stranger on the street. He is a fine example of a minister with a true heart for all God's children.

This book of daily devotions will give the reader a clear indication of the author's heart and will serve to encourage all those who begin their day with the Word and the accompanying exhortation. I recommend this book without reservation to those who desire to start their day on a positive note.

Russell & Judy McCollough
Four Corners Ministries
Roseville, CA

Thank you, Lord God, for blessing me to have a friend in Pastor John Weigelt. He is a true inspiration to many through his Pastoral teachings and his Spirit filled literary work which inspires and encourages many of God's people looking for a positive way to start their day, with Scripture references and inspirational messages from the heart of a True Man of God!!! John Weigelt, Husband, Father, Pastor/Teacher, Author and my dear friend!!!

I highly recommend his book, "24 Karat" Daily Nuggets of Inspiration.

Ron & Marsha Reed
True Faith Christian Fellowship
Carson, CA

I have found that a timely word is food for the soul. That is what I have found so often in these devotions. I have been privileged to be a recipient of these daily devotions even before their publication. It has been like manna from heaven. Spiritual insight given simply, sincerely, and daily. Who could ask for more!

Joe Carrillo
Band of Brothers Ministerial Fellowship
www.bobfellowship.org
Sacramento, CA

I have known Pastor John Weigelt for over fifteen years. In all the years that I have been a part of his congregation, I can say that faithfulness to God's Word is perhaps his greatest quality. He does not stand before his church and give "opinions." Rather, he proclaims the true account (and hermeneutically sound) of the word of God and of His Son, Jesus Christ.

As with his first book, I am fully confident that Pastor John has filled every page of this book with spiritual truth and godly wisdom from the Scriptures. It is my honor to be able to serve under him at South Bay New Life Christian Center and receive the wealth of God's Word that he brings each week. It is my sincere hope and prayer that all who read this book will better get to know who Pastor John Weigelt is and the heart that he has for the Lord. I fully endorse these treasured gems that he provides from his daily walk with God.

Paul Herbert
Minister, New Life Christian Center

DAILY JEWELS

1. THE NIGHT SHIFT

"Praise the Lord, all you servants of the Lord who minister by night in the house of the Lord. Lift up your hands in the sanctuary and praise the Lord." Psalm 134:1-2 NIV

When I looked at the history behind this Psalm, I discovered that there was, according to what I read, a "graveyard shift" or night shift in the Temple of God back in those days. Some of the priests would be assigned to guard or stand watch in the temple throughout the night. The Psalmist seems to be encouraging those tired and sleepy servants of the Lord to "Wake up! Be alert! Lift up your hands and Praise the Lord!"

It seems to me that many people are just plain tired these days. More and more people are working weekends and nights on their jobs. And they are worn out. [Note: I worked the night shift for about 16 years on my previous job]. Let's pray more fervently for those who are "consumed" by their work schedules - pray for supernatural strength to lift up their hands and hearts and voices so they can effectively "Praise the Lord"!

2. THE TABLET OF YOUR HEART

"My son, keep my words and store up my commands within you. Keep my commands and you will live; guard my teachings as the apple of your eye. Bind them on your fingers; write them on the tablet of your heart." Proverbs 7:1-3 NIV

KEEP, STORE UP, GUARD - These words are action words (verbs) and are often used with things of value. In this Proverb the valuable things are WORDS, COMMANDS, and TEACHINGS. The phrase that stood out in my mind is, "write them on the tablet of your heart".

To "write" something on the "tablet" of your heart refers to committing something to memory. Another term is to "etch" or "carve" in our memory or consciousness. This is the way of learning. So, how much of God's Words, Commands, and Teachings have you committed to memory? Don't confess, "I can't do it" or, " I just can't memorize anything", because you do remember the things that are most important to you.

3. DON'T GET STUCK IN A RUT
"Instruct the wise and they will be wiser still; teach the righteous and they will add to their learning." Proverbs 9:9 NIV

Have you ever been "stuck in a rut"? It's not a pleasant feeling. Maybe you feel like you are spinning your wheels and going nowhere. What do you do?

This Proverb is an invitation to grow and advance through instruction and teaching. Notice that this growth is pointing toward those who are already wise and righteous. Why do you think that is? It's because they desire to grow. The wicked, the foolish, and the mockers want nothing to do with receiving instruction.

Don't get stuck in a rut by refusing to be taught. 2 Peter 3:18 says, *"But grow in the grace and knowledge of our Lord and Savior Jesus Christ."*

4. GUILTY CONSCIENCE vs CLEAR CONSCIENCE

"What the wicked dread will overtake them; what the righteous desire will be granted."   Proverbs 10:24 NIV

What a wise contrast! The "wicked" and the "righteous"; "dread" and "desire". It would seem that both kinds of people could have both things they dread and things they desire. However, the Wisdom of God reveals that wicked people are aware of the consequences of their wrong-doing . . . and they dread the outcome. They live with guilty consciences.

On the other hand, the righteous have no evil intent regarding their actions or desires - so they have nothing to regret or dread. They have a clear conscience and a pure heart. Having a clear conscience is a great reward.

5. NIGHT VISION

"If I say, "Surely the darkness will hide me and the light become night around me," even the darkness will not be dark to you; the night will shine like the day, for darkness is as light to you."
Psalm 139:11-12 NIV

After David asked the question, "Where can I flee from your presence", he answered his own question in this Psalm. In the verses above, David mentions "darkness" and that God is not affected by the dark. It's as if God has "Night Vision". Most crime, violence, sin, and hiding takes place under the cover of darkness - at least it used to be that way.

David continues to say that darkness, or night, will shine like the day - or will be illuminated. So, let's not think that we can ever isolate or hide ourselves, our actions, or thoughts from God. We are always in His light and His ever-watching eyes see it all.

6. LIFTING WEIGHTS
"Anxiety weighs down the heart, but a kind word cheers it up."
Proverbs 12:25 NIV

According to Wikipedia, Anxiety is an emotion characterized by an unpleasant state of inner turmoil. It is the subjectively unpleasant feelings of dread over anticipated events. Anxiety is not the same as fear.

The emotional state human beings can be seriously detrimental to their health and their well-being, especially if it is in turmoil. This Proverb says that anxiety "weighs down the heart" but this heaviness of heart can be relieved by kind words.

We never know what others are going through, or how they are thinking. Lord, help us to be more sensitive toward others, and help us find words of kindness to comfort them. Help us to be "weight lifters".

7. WHERE'S YOUR HEAD?
"Sovereign Lord, my strong deliverer, you shield my head in the day of battle."   Psalm 140:7 NIV

You have probably heard the following phrases: "Get your head in the game"; "My head is all messed up"; "Keep your head on straight"; or "I can't wrap my head around it".

Our head is so valuable. All our thinking and reasoning is done in our head - and located in our head is our brain. The brain is an organ that serves as the center of the nervous system and it is the most complex organ in a vertebrate's body.

When David wrote, "You shield my head in the day of battle", he was familiar with doing physical battle with enemies. He knew the importance of a helmet for protection. In addition, he knew the importance of having a right mind - or confidence in the One who was his Protector - when being attacked by his enemies. WHERE IS YOUR HEAD?

8. NO CATTLE, NO CROPS
"Where there are no oxen, the manger is empty, but from the strength of an ox come abundant harvests." Proverbs 14:4 NIV

This verse seems to be a bit odd in the midst of the preceding and following verses. The Message Bible translation puts it this way, "No cattle, no crops."

This verse, however, has always stood out in my mind. It has taught me a valuable lesson. A very long time ago I found myself complaining about people leaving the church dirty - this was while I was cleaning the church. I was grumbling and complaining. I don't recall how I connected this verse to church cleaning but here's the thought . . . or revelation: "No people, no mess. No mess, no people, no church".

Thank God for the people in our church. Though they might, or will, make a mess, and someone needs to clean up that mess, with no people there would be no "church". I'm not trying to compare people with oxen or cattle, but without the people in our churches we would never have anyone to minister to, fellowship with, or to disciple. There would be no growth of the "Body".

9. THE RIGHT ONE TO COMPLAIN TO

"I cry aloud to the Lord; I lift up my voice to the Lord for mercy. I pour out before him my complaint; before him I tell my trouble. When my spirit grows faint within me, it is you who watch over my way."
Psalm 142:1-3 NIV

King David wrote these words. David was a mighty king and a mighty warrior . . . but he was also a humble man who knew his weakness. David had many mighty warriors in his army to protect him - but he knew the mightiest Warrior of all, the LORD GOD.

David said that he "cried aloud" and "lifted up his voice" and poured out his complaints to the LORD. He knew his strength and protection did not come from his own skills or from his mighty army. When David's life was in danger, he knew the right One to complain to.

Who do you complain to when things in your life are falling apart, or when you are attacked on every side with problems? Pour out your complaint, tell all your problems to the Lord - not to everyone else. It is the Lord who watches over your way.

10. GOOD MEDICINE

"A cheerful heart is good medicine, but a crushed spirit dries up the bones."   Proverbs 17:22 NIV

Just because someone seems happy on the outside (we used call that a "happy-go-lucky" person) that doesn't mean they have a cheerful heart. How many famous, and really funny, comedians have you known that have either committed suicide or died from drug overdoses or were alcoholics?

Being funny doesn't mean everything is at peace or cheerful on the inside. Many people have a crushed spirit and just "mask" the hurt and pain with humor. But a truly cheerful heart comes from being content and satisfied - a heart that is free from anger & bitterness, envy & jealousy, pride & ego.

Give yourself a "heart checkup". While you are at it, check your bones too - are they dried up? Of course, I am speaking metaphorically - but is your heart truly cheerful? A cheerful heart is GOOD MEDICINE and that comes from having a great relationship with God, our Creator, our Heavenly Father.

11. WHEN YOU ARE DOWN, LOOK UP
"The Lord upholds all who fall and lifts up all who are bowed down." Psalm 145:14 NIV

I remembered an old saying my Dad would tell me - and it's NOT a good saying, but I remember it: "Never kick a man when he's down . . . only when he starts to get up." Isn't that like what we see in the world?

Well, in this Psalm of David we are reminded that the LORD will hold up those who fall. He knows how frail we are at times (even though we don't think we are). The LORD lifts up and encourages those who are bowed down under the heavy load of sorrows and worries and sin. Another saying of my Dad was: "When you are down, look up and see who's holding your hand." Now that's worth remembering.

12. READ THE INSTRUCTIONS
"Stop listening to instruction, my son, and you will stray from the words of knowledge." Proverbs 19:27 NIV

Instructions - aren't they wonderful? Almost everything today comes with a set of instructions. But, how many of us actually read them?

I remember when I was very young, my Dad bought me a "Visible V-8 Engine" for Christmas (a plastic model). I hurried to put it together - I had put many model cars together before. When I had completed putting the engine together, it wouldn't work . . . and I got mad. My Dad asked me if I read the instructions. What? "I don't need no stinking instructions!"

Well, he made me take it all apart and read the instructions first, and then put it together. THAT DID THE TRICK! So, I discovered the importance of reading and following instructions. The writer of this Proverb says that if we stop listening to instructions we will stray from the words of knowledge. How true that is. Pay attention to "The Instruction Manual" - you will be wise if you do.

13. NO PAIN, NO GAIN
"Blows and wounds scrub away evil, and beatings purge the inmost being."   Proverbs 20:30 NIV

No one that I know enjoys being "beat up" in life. We usually want things to be calm and peaceful - no problems or attacks. However, the writer of this Proverb, Solomon, says that beatings and wounds are beneficial to cleanse our inner being. A popular saying found plastered on gym walls is, "No pain, no gain." But many of us like to think, "No pain, NO PAIN!"

So, when life's difficulties and challenges arise in our life, remember the benefits - especially for believers. The Lord is trying to reveal the wrong in us, correct what is corrupt, and purge the putrid.

Also, Psalm 119 says, *"Before I was afflicted, I went astray, but now I obey your word"* (verse 67). And verse 71 says, *"It was good for me to be afflicted so that I might learn your decrees."*

14. JUST THE RIGHT SIZE

"Praise the Lord. How good it is to sing praises to our God, how pleasant and fitting to praise him!" Psalm 147:1 NIV

The word "fitting" stood out to me in this verse. Have you ever tried to wear a pair of shoes that were too small? It can be uncomfortable and even painful. Or, have you worn clothes that were too tight or too loose? It's not a very pleasant experience, is it?

The Psalmist here is focused on our PRAISE to the Lord. Praise can be done in a variety of ways, but he states here that singing praises to God is good - it is pleasant and pleasing to Him. Then he says it is "fitting" to praise Him. In other words, it is becoming, it fits perfectly like a glove, it's just the right size. Notice that there is no mention of how it sounds or if it's in the right key.

So, don't worry about how you sound when singing praises to the Lord, just do it because your praise is always the right size.

15. RICHES OR REPUTATION?

"A good name is more desirable than great riches; to be esteemed is better than silver or gold." Proverbs 22:1 NIV

The Message Bible says this: *"A sterling reputation is better than striking it rich; a gracious spirit is better than money in the bank."*

What do people think when your name is brought up? What will they remember about you when you are gone? I don't think they will remember how much money you had (or didn't have). I believe they will remember your character and how you treated them.

What do you think of when you hear the name JESUS? All the great and awesome things He had done? Or how He loves you? Or His mercy and compassion and forgiveness?

What will follow you, what will be remembered, what will "stand out" . . . your riches or your reputation?

16. GOD DESERVES ALL OUR PRAISE

"Praise the Lord. Praise God in his sanctuary; praise him in his mighty heavens. Praise him for his acts of power; praise him for his surpassing greatness."   Psalm 150:1-2 NIV

"Let everything that has breath praise the Lord. Praise the Lord." Psalm 150:6 NIV

Our God deserves our praise. He does far more than we know - He is at work openly as well as behind the scenes. So, don't stop short in your praises. Praise Him for the things you don't see yet. Praise Him for what you hope for.

As long as you have breath, praise the Lord with it. After all, He gave it to you at birth - give it back to Him.

17. RELIEVE YOURSELF OF RETALIATION

"If your enemy is hungry, give him food to eat; if he is thirsty, give him water to drink. In doing this, you will heap burning coals on his head, and the Lord will reward you."   Proverbs 25:21-22 NIV

We can take a huge load off of our mind if we allow the Lord to make our "enemies" (those who don't like us or are angry with us) feel guilty. We sometimes spend a lot of emotional energy maintaining our anger toward someone or licking our wounds/hurts.

This Psalm reminds us that as we let go of our retaliation mindset, and do good toward our enemies, the burning pain of guilt will be, not gently applied, but "heaped on them" automatically.

I believe I read that Abraham Lincoln is credited for saying, "The best way to destroy an enemy is to make him a friend." So, Relieve yourself of Retaliation - Pay, don't Repay.

Stop saying, "I'll get even with . . . ". Remember, when you want to "get even" with someone you are wanting to be on the same level with them. Be better than that!

18. LIPSTICK ON A PIG . . .
"Like a coating of silver dross on earthenware are fervent lips with an evil heart."   Proverbs 26:23 NIV

Have you ever made pottery is school or as a hobby? I have done that a few times. We used regular clay and shaped it into an object. Then, after it dried for a time, we painted it with something called glaze. It didn't look very good or impressive at first. But after putting it into an oven (kiln) for a few hours, that glaze became colorful and turned that object into something beautiful. Though it looked valuable to the eye, there was still regular, inexpensive clay underneath.

The wise author of this Proverb reminds us that fervent, persuasive talk from an evil heart (impure motives) is just a coverup. It may sound good and pleasant to the ears - but watch out, be careful to examine the intent. Like the old adage, "You can put lipstick on a pig, but it's still a pig."

19. FRIEND OR FOE?
"Wounds from a friend can be trusted, but an enemy multiplies kisses."
Proverbs 27:6 NIV

Thank God for real friends who will correct us, scold us, and be real with us. It may not feel good and it may downright hurt. The motive behind their honesty is to help us see our blind spots.

People who don't really care about us will never take the time to shape our character - but they may try to "sweet talk" their way into our lives for selfish reasons.

Look for and keep those real friends in your life - and be that kind of friend to others as well.

20. FAVOR ALL AROUND
"Surely, Lord, you bless the righteous; you surround them with your favor as with a shield." Psalm 5:12 NIV

Think back of how many times you were unexpectedly blessed. Sometimes we don't even realize that God's favor was at work. When things don't go exactly the way you planned, when you are inconveniently delayed, or you get interrupted in the middle of your business, God is up to something. Stop and see things from God's perspective.

If you are a child of God, He has declared you "righteous". And it's not because of your good looks, skills, intelligence, or good deeds. You are declared righteous only because you have placed your faith in the work of Jesus Christ. Because of this, God shields you on every side.

21. WHAT'S IN YOUR HEART?
"Lord my God, I take refuge in you; save and deliver me from all who pursue me, or they will tear me apart like a lion and rip me to pieces with no one to rescue me." Psalm 7:1-2 NIV

These words were written by a king - King David. We read from the Bible history ("His Story") that David was a mighty warrior. This Psalm doesn't sound like a "mighty warrior" wrote it. However, we do see beneath the surface and into David's heart.

Many, many people either seem great or powerful on the outside but are wimps in reality - down deep. They put on a good "mask" or facade for others to see. Some "bullies" are like that - until someone calls their bluff. Others really are strong and powerful, but they are tender and humble on the inside.

So, which are you? Do you openly try to display your power and boldness, or do you really know where your strength and protection comes from? Don't be an "actor" (Greek = hupokrités, or hypocrite).

22. LISTEN TO THE VOICE OF WISDOM
"Out in the open wisdom calls aloud, she raises her voice in the public square; on top of the wall she cries out, at the city gate she makes her speech . . ." Proverbs 1:20-21 NIV

Godly wisdom is not difficult to find - it does not lurk in the dark shadows of back alleys. Nor is it buried in deep caverns. So, how do we find this wisdom that can guide our life? The writer, Solomon, states that Wisdom is out in the open, available to all who will "tune in" to its voice.

The real question is, who desires to hear Godly Wisdom versus worldly wisdom or philosophy? The seventh verse of this Proverb says that "fools despise wisdom and discipline". To the natural mind, the wisdom of the world appears more attractive because it seems to make sense. Godly Wisdom, on the other hand, is supernatural, far above and beyond our understanding. So, choose not to be foolish - listen to God's Wisdom and really start living.

23. A MIGHTY FORTRESS IS OUR GOD
"The Lord is a refuge for the oppressed, a stronghold in times of trouble."   Psalm 9:9 NIV

I remember when I was a child making a fort in my room. Usually I would make it out of blankets and sheets from my bed. Maybe you have done something similar. I would pretend to hide from my enemies (usually Indians - because of watching cowboy movies) and feel safe as long as I would be surrounded by those thin covers.

In Psalm 9, David paints for us a vivid picture of a "stronghold" or a place to hide from enemies. But this place of hiding was not made of thin coverings that couldn't stop a fly from entering - it is the LORD Himself, strong and mighty.

When we are faced with our "enemies", whether they are actual people, or health issues, or financial issues, or imaginary issues we seem to worry about, picture yourself running into a huge, strong, impenetrable fortress. That fortress is THE LORD. Then, the feeling of safety will comfort you.

24. THE BEAUTY OF GOD'S CREATION

"By wisdom the Lord laid the earth's foundations, by understanding he set the heavens in place; by his knowledge the watery depths were divided, and the clouds let drop the dew."   Proverbs 3:19-20 NIV

There are times when I like to look at various things that have been created. And there are so many I have not yet seen. But every time I travel to the Hawaiian Islands I feel a sense of awe, especially when standing at the base of a 400 foot waterfall, or cautiously peering into a blowhole just before it spews, or standing atop a cliff overlooking the ocean contemplating jumping into the water, or viewing the steep and rugged mountains, or capturing a glimpse of a million stars glowing against a pitch black sky.

These, and many other wondrous sights throughout the world, are not random developments. The heavens and the earth are a product of God's Wisdom, Understanding, and Knowledge. How magnificent and awe-inspiring it is to think about God's creative plan and purpose - and how He created our eyes to enjoy the beauty of His creation, His Masterpiece. Isn't our God AWESOME?

25. THE HEART OF THE MATTER

"Above all else, guard your heart, for everything you do flows from it." Proverbs 4:23 NIV

Have you ever experienced a "broken heart"? Almost everyone has at some point in their life. It hurts! Now, we understand this terminology not as a physical breaking of the organ that pumps blood throughout our body, but as a deep emotional hurt. These hurts can destroy us - and we in turn can hurt others.

Our "heart" - in the context of this verse - is the center, the core, of our very being, the seat of all our emotions. Why does Solomon tell us to "guard" our heart, and how do we do that? In the preceding and the following verses, Solomon focuses on the importance of gaining

Wisdom and Understanding. Wisdom, God's Wisdom, brings understanding of life into the center of our being. From this "treasure vault" flows all that we do, think, and feel - it governs us.

Let's make sure our hearts are full of Godly Treasure (Wisdom) which comes from God's Word. And guard it as if our life depended on it . . . because it does!

26. LORD, SHOW US YOUR WAYS

"Help, Lord, for no one is faithful anymore; those who are loyal have vanished from the human race. Everyone lies to their neighbor; they flatter with their lips but harbor deception in their hearts. May the Lord silence all flattering lips and every boastful tongue— those who say, "By our tongues we will prevail; our own lips will defend us—who is lord over us?"" Psalm 12:1-4 NIV

Wow! Was King David talking about the days he lived in - or ours? Obviously, he was referring to his day, but it sure sounds familiar. Aren't we experiencing some of the same behaviors, especially in our government? Is this shocking to you? Well, nothing shocks God. Sinful human behavior will always be the same - there is nothing new under the sun.

What can we, who believe in, and trust in, and follow God's instructions, do? We ought to be more purposeful and intense in knowing what God's Word teaches us, and then obey that teaching. We need to make sure we are keeping our eyes on HIM and not on "political ideals", or humanistic reasoning.

As King David wrote: "Help, LORD". Oh, how we need HIM.

27. WRESTLING IN PRAYER

"How long, Lord? Will you forget me forever? How long will you hide your face from me? How long must I wrestle with my thoughts and day after day have sorrow in my heart? How long will my enemy triumph over me?"   Psalm 13:1-2 NIV

Do you ever find yourself praying as David prayed here? Do you ever question God and agonize over your thoughts about why HE hasn't answered your prayer? It's almost like a wrestling match, trying to pin God down to an answer. Many of us have probably been guilty of this.

Prayer is a conversation with God, our loving Father, our Creator and Savior. We must realize that God never ignores even our simplest prayer because He never minimizes our requests - or what we THINK WE NEED. When we pray, we must pray in faith and with confidence that God knows exactly what we need - and when.

At the conclusion of this Psalm, David changed his tune - he admitted to himself that he trusted in God's unfailing love, even when the answer was not yet seen. It's as if he conceded his wrestling match, his struggling prayer, and "exposed his shoulders to the mat". PINNED BY GOD!

28. GOD IS LOOKING

"The Lord looks down from heaven on all mankind to see if there are any who understand, any who seek God."   Psalm 14:2 NIV

What does the LORD see when He looks down from heaven today? What does He see in mankind - His created beings? Doesn't the Bible tell us that nature itself worships Him? Isaiah 55:12 speaks of the mountains and hills bursting into song and the trees of the field clapping their hands. So, what does He see the people doing?

Picture in your mind - right now - what does He see you doing? Are you full of "busyness", are you preparing for a day of activity or pleasure, or are you worrying about your situation? Or does the Lord see you praying and praising and seeking His presence? Does He see you reading and studying His Word? Does He see you "being Jesus" toward someone who needs a savior?

Now, ask yourself this question: "Am I doing what I'm doing just because God might be watching? Or am I doing it because I love HIM?"

29. NO COMPARISON
"Choose my instruction instead of silver, knowledge rather than choice gold, for wisdom is more precious than rubies, and nothing you desire can compare with her."   Proverbs 8:10-11 NIV

The "voice" speaking here is Wisdom. And Wisdom is pleading with all mankind to choose instruction and knowledge because of its great value. We are told that Wisdom is of greater value, more precious, than rubies. Rubies are worth between $1000 a $3000 per carat - depending on size, color, and origin. Diamonds are a worth a bit more. And the price of gold and silver is always fluctuating.

One thing that never fluctuates is the value of Godly Wisdom. Nothing you could ever desire can be compared with the value of Wisdom. So, what are you desiring in your life? What "things" do you place a high value on? Choose Godly Wisdom - choose Godly Instruction and Knowledge.

30. WHO ARE YOU LOOKING AT?
"I keep my eyes always on the Lord. With him at my right hand, I will not be shaken." Psalm 16:8 NIV

In Psalm 14, it says that the Lord looks down from heaven on us. And in today's Psalm, David says that he kept his eyes on the Lord. I remember a friend telling me of an old Country song titled "I Was Lookin' Back to See if You Were Lookin' Back to See if I Was Lookin' Back to See if You Were Lookin' Back At Me." I thought he was joking until he showed me the record album.

That's a lot of looking. But just think of the anticipation in looking intently to see if you are being looked at. David said he ALWAYS kept his eyes on the Lord - that's where his strength and encouragement came from. Are we doing the same? Or, do we get distracted by "life's stuff" and turn our eyes away from the Lord? When we do, we loose focus and the "stuff" gains a greater importance and a greater power in our life. "Turn Your Eyes Upon Jesus; Look Full in His Wonderful Face. And the Things of Earth Will Grow Strangely Dim; In the Light of His Glory and Grace." (an old, old hymn)

31. GOD SEES AND JUDGES CORRECTLY
"Let my vindication come from you; may your eyes see what is right."
Psalm 17:2 NIV

Have you ever wondered what other people think of you? I'm sure it has crossed your mind a few times . . . every day. Sometimes we get so caught up in worrying about what someone else thinks that we are afraid to be ourselves.

On the other hand, have you ever judged someone else's actions or behavior? From your own perspective you are right - but maybe not from their perspective. You don't see or know the whole situation.

To insure you have peace of mind, pray as David prayed, "Let my vindication come from You." David knew that God sees everything, and HE sees things correctly. So, make sure your focus is on pleasing God and not others.

32. GOD IS ALL THAT!
"I love you, Lord, my strength. The Lord is my rock, my fortress and my deliverer; my God is my rock, in whom I take refuge, my shield and the horn of my salvation, my stronghold."   Psalm 18:1-2 NIV

King David wrote this song to the Lord when the Lord had delivered him from the hand of his enemies. When reading this entire Psalm, you can see all the various ways David's foes attacked him. In spite of all that, and in light of the way God delivered him, David used some very descriptive words to describe God - His Deliverer: "Rock; Fortress; Deliverer; Shield; Horn (strength); and Stronghold".

When we look at all the challenges and difficulties in our life, they don't even come close to what David had experienced - at least mine don't. But, if we would only focus on how David describes our God instead of how we might describe our problems, we should be encouraged . . . if we truly believe. Our God is "Rock Solid". He is our "Protector", He is our "Strength", He is our "SAVIOR"! AMEN!

33. WITH OR WITHOUT WORDS, DECLARE GOD'S GOODNESS
"The heavens declare the glory of God; the skies proclaim the work of his hands. Day after day they pour forth speech; night after night they reveal knowledge. They have no speech, they use no words; no sound is heard from them."   Psalm 19:1-3 NIV

When you meditate on these verses, a sense of awe seems to descend from heaven. God's Glory and His activity is being revealed from the skies around us. We hear no words, but we seem to understand the "language" or communication.

Though it is important for us to communicate the Gospel, the love of God, to others around us by using our words, it is of equal importance to demonstrate the Gospel by our actions and lifestyle. In the book of James, chapter 2, we are told that just saying to a brother or sister without clothes or food, "be warm and well fed", but not actually helping them, is of little or no value. So, declare the Good News, the love of Christ, with words and without words as well.

34. THE LORD GIVES VICTORY

"Now this I know: The Lord gives victory to his anointed. He answers him from his heavenly sanctuary with the victorious power of his right hand."   Psalm 20:6 NIV

David, the author of this Psalm, was a mighty warrior as well as Israel's greatest king. He could have written volumes about his achievements. Instead, he wrote of the "origin of all power and victory". And look at what he claimed - "Now this I know"!

We talk about, and we sing about, God's Power and His Victories, but do we really, really believe and KNOW beyond all doubt that God gives us victory from His powerful hand? If we do know this - why would we ever worry or fear our circumstances? THE LORD GIVES VICTORY!

35. LORD, YOU KNOW

"Each heart knows its own bitterness, and no one else can share its joy." Proverbs 14:10 NIV

"Even in laughter the heart may ache, and rejoicing may end in grief." Proverbs 14:13 NIV

I find it odd that so many great comedians, past and possibly present, suffer from depression and lack of self-esteem. Many have committed suicide or overindulged in drugs & alcohol - trying to kill the pain deep inside.

One thing this tells us is that we can never fully know the hurt or bitterness - or true joy - that someone else has inside. Their outer actions may give us a clue, but only that person really knows for sure. But Lord, You know - so teach us to approach each person we may see with caution and care. Help us to realize that what we see on the surface may just be a mask for danger underneath.

36. MAY THE WORDS OF OUR MOUTH BE ACCEPTABLE
"The heart of the righteous weighs its answers, but the mouth of the wicked gushes evil."   Proverbs 16:28 NIV

Have you ever been told by a parent or a teacher, "Think before you speak." I know I have heard that many times - and I often say that to myself. There is a lot of wisdom in that saying. How many arguments have been avoided, how many insults have been quenched by using this simple, but effective advice?

I found a fitting quote by Jhiess Krieg: "Please, God, make my words today sweet and tender, for tomorrow I may have to eat them." Would you say "Yum" or would you say "Yuck"?

37. ARE YOU HUNGRY ENOUGH?
"The appetite of laborers works for them; their hunger drives them on."
Proverbs 16:26 NIV

What motivates you? What increases your desire for more? In this Proverb, it is the laborer's appetite for food that motivates him to work.

Before I continue my thoughts on motivation, today's reading in the book of Psalms is chapter 23 - a very familiar reading, and rich in imagery. But, how many of us have memorized this Psalm? Have we understood the value in what it reveals? There is an abundance of "food for thought" in Psalm 23. So, my question for us today is: How hungry are we for the Word of God, and does that hunger - or appetite - drive us on to read, memorize, and meditate on God's precious Word?

38. WHAT ARE YOU HEARING?
"A wicked person listens to deceitful lips; a liar pays attention to a destructive tongue."   Proverbs 17:4 NIV

Have you ever caught yourself listening intently to someone speaking negatively about someone else? It's easy to do if we are not careful. Just think, there are no proven facts, just personal opinions. It's a one-sided conversation. This Proverb states that a wicked person and a liar does this.

OUCH. I don't want to be called or be thought of as a liar, or wicked. So, let's be on our guard, be cautious of who and what we lend our ears to (remember that line from the play "Julius Caesar: "Friends, Romans, countrymen, lend me your ears."). Are you using your ears to hear beauty and blessings - or to soak up deceit and destruction?

39. DON'T REMEMBER BUT REMEMBER

*"Do not remember the sins of my youth and my rebellious ways;
according to your love remember me, for you, Lord, are good."*
Psalm 25:7 NIV

Here's some shocking news - I did some awful and sinful things when I
was young. I was even rebellious. Such is the life of almost everyone -
even King David.

David's Prayer to the Lord in this Psalm is twofold: 1) "Do not
remember", and 2) "Remember". In other words, he is asking God to
forget (not remember) his sinful and rebellious ways as a youth, but to
not forget (remember) him.

Here we can see a wonderful way that God sees us - with a separation
between the person and their behavior. Could this be where the saying,
"Love the sinner but hate the sin" comes from? Where would we all be if
God rejected us, "remembered" our sins, and held them against us
forever?

40. HELPING THE POOR

*"Whoever is kind to the poor lends to the Lord, and he will reward them
for what they have done."*   Proverbs 19:17 NIV

Wherever we look we see poor people. Some are homeless, some we
see begging for money, and some seem to have a lot at first glance, but
are actually struggling to make ends meet. Some are poor because
their lives have just fallen apart - but others are poor due to their own
foolishness and greed.

On the other hand, we know that there are also a lot of "scammers" and
deceivers posing as being poor. So, we need to use caution and
discernment when we want to help. I am usually a "sucker" for their
stories and have been fooled a few times. Have you?

Let's be careful, but not calloused when it comes to helping those in need. In any case, this Proverb tells us that when we help out or give to the poor, we are LENDING TO THE LORD - not to the person. And the Lord always REWARDS us (over and above), not just pays us back.

41. SAFE AND SECURE - NO FEAR
"The Lord is my light and my salvation— whom shall I fear? The Lord is the stronghold of my life— of whom shall I be afraid?"
Psalm 27:1 NIV

We sometimes sing this song in our church during the time of worship. It encourages us when we might be experiencing life's challenges. Instead of becoming disabled by fear, we are reminded to trust in the Lord - He is our stronghold. Other versions of the Bible use the word "refuge" or "fortress" or "strength".

When difficult times come our way that might cause us to fear (finances, health, etc.), allow the words of this Psalm, and others, to "paint a picture" in your mind of a strong, sturdy Fort with thick walls. Picture yourself running into this Fort for protection. Picture in your mind a bright light inside where you can clearly see the Lord, your Savior, there to protect you. In this place there is no fear and no worries - only peace and calm.

42. MY HEART LEAPS FOR JOY!
"The Lord is my strength and my shield; my heart trusts in him, and he helps me. My heart leaps for joy, and with my song I praise him."
Psalm 28:7 NIV

Have you ever had your heart "leap for joy"? Maybe it was your first attraction to someone, or winning an event, or receiving an award. Maybe it was your firstborn child. Something or someone caused a joy that you can't describe . . . remember that feeling?

King David expressed this feeling in this Psalm - but it wasn't for a great victory over an enemy or for his wife (or wives). It was because he trusted in the LORD'S strength and protection. Imagine the relationship David had with God! He wasn't a perfect man, but he had an awesome "love affair" with the God of creation, the Mighty King of all. Does this describe your relationship with a God?

43. ZEAL FOR FEAR

"Do not let your heart envy sinners, but always be zealous for the fear of the Lord."   Proverbs 23:17 NIV

Fear is something that comes naturally to us. Things that we know are dangerous, things that hurt, and things we are unsure of, are just a few of the things that cause us to fear. So why does this author (Solomon) tell us (his audience) to fear the Lord with zeal?

The dictionary's definition of ZEAL is: fervor for a person, cause, or object; eager desire or endeavor; enthusiastic diligence; ardor. I get "zeal for the Lord" - but to have zeal for the fear of the Lord? Why??

Loving the Lord but fearing His wrath will keep us from a life of sin. Also, Solomon tells us that the fear of the Lord is the beginning of Wisdom.

44. GOD HEARS OUR CRY

"Praise be to the Lord, for he showed me the wonders of his love when I was in a city under siege. In my alarm I said, "I am cut off from your sight!" Yet you heard my cry for mercy when I called to you for help." Psalm 31:21-22 NIV

Many of the Psalms written by David were written from his personal encounters with his enemies who were trying to take his life. David didn't hide any of his emotions when he wrote these songs, or Psalms.

In this Psalm, David touches on the wonders of God's love being revealed when he felt like he was "cut off" from God's sight. It's almost like a child being lost in a busy shopping mall or stadium, separated from their parent. In panic and despair, the child cries out "Mommy" or "Daddy"! Can you almost feel the sensation? But then, the child sees their parent racing toward them, and a great feeling of overwhelming relief STOPS the fear! The child's voice was heard!

Similarly, the Lord hears our cry when we are desperate, as He did for David, and He comes quickly on the scene. In His mercy He shows the wonder of His great Love for us and quiets our fears.

45. DO NOT ASSUME

"Blessed is the one whose transgressions are forgiven, whose sins are covered. Blessed is the one whose sin the Lord does not count against them and in whose spirit is no deceit." Psalm 32:1-2 NIV

Many of us know the problems we experience when we assume something. Just because we "believe" something is correct, that doesn't actually or automatically make it correct.

In this Psalm, the author – David - didn't assume sins and transgressions were automatically forgiven by God. No, we need to read the following verses especially verse 5. What David expressed is that he acknowledged his sin and confessed it before God. So, let's not assume that God automatically forgives our mistakes, faults, rebellion, or sins. We must first acknowledge that we are in error - make no attempt to deceive the Lord. Then, we must confess our sin to God. The result? Forgiveness and Blessings from God, and a restored relationship with Him.

46. FITTING AND APPROPRIATE
"Sing joyfully to the Lord, you righteous; it is fitting for the upright to praise him."   Psalm 33:1 NIV

Not every event or function that you attend requires the same type of clothing. For example, you wouldn't go the the gym in a tuxedo - neither would you attend a formal dinner in your workout gear. You would want to, and are expected to, dress appropriately and look presentable.

In a similar way, using this application, this Psalm states that it is fitting for God's people to give God praise. The Amplified Bible uses the words *"becoming and appropriate"*. Not only is praising God an appropriate and expected behavior, but HOW it is to be done is the focus in this verse. We are told to *"sing joyfully"* to the Lord. That is the appropriate and presentable way to praise our God.

47. THE AROMA OF A FRIEND
"Perfume and incense bring joy to the heart, and the pleasantness of a friend springs from their heartfelt advice."   Proverbs 27:9 NIV

There is something mysterious about our sense of smell. A fragrant aroma, like perfume or cologne, does something strange to us. Have you ever, when you were young, received a letter in the mail from someone you were fond of, or in love with? And the pages of that letter were saturated with a scent of perfume (not an overwhelming Avon perfume that grandma would wear). That sweet fragrance somehow put your mind in a pleasant place as you read the words of that letter. It seemed that those written words would then saturate your mind.

The pleasantness of friends - good friends - is compared in this Proverb to the aroma that an expensive perfume or incense exudes. Good friends are valuable, make sure you are surrounded with a few - or more. In addition, make sure you are a good friend to someone else.

48. I GOT THIS!
"Those who trust in themselves are fools, but those who walk in wisdom are kept safe."   Proverbs 28:26 NIV

When minor challenges arise in our life - no big deal - do we forget to ask God for help? We wouldn't want to bother Him with such trivial circumstances. No, we'll save the bigger problems for Him to handle. We are told, "Don't sweat the small stuff."

It's at these times that we are most like the one written about in this Proverb - "*those who trust in themselves*". Actually, no problem is too small to trust God with. We know, don't we, that our God is more powerful than our biggest challenge - but He is also bigger than our smallest problems. Trusting God, and not in ourselves, with all things is called Wisdom.

49. THE KINGDOM IS NOT AN EXCLUSIVE CLUB
"How priceless is your unfailing love! Both high and low among men find refuge in the shadow of your wings."   Psalm 36:7 NIV

Did you know that Disneyland (So. California) has an Exclusive Club? It's called Club 33 and it is located in the New Orleans Square. There are many perks for its members, as do other exclusive clubs. I am told that to become a member of Club 33 there is an initiation fee of $25,000 per person and an annual membership fee of $10,000. That's a good reason for me to not be a member.

Aren't you glad that there is no "exclusive club" in God's Kingdom? In the Psalm today, we read that both the high and low (upper-class and lower-class people) can find refuge in the Lord. Now that's a Club I feel comfortable in. We are all one body with no favoritism.

50. THE LORD LAUGHS AT THE WICKED
"The wicked plot against the righteous and gnash their teeth at them; but the Lord laughs at the wicked, for he knows their day is coming." Psalm 37:12-13 NIV

Years ago, I saw a picture of Jesus laughing. I thought that was interesting because most pictures I had ever seen before that time showed Jesus with a very serious look on His face. Now, I realize there are no actual pictures of Jesus, but the one, or ones, of Him laughing help us picture in our minds a different view of Jesus. [For fun, do a search on the internet for "Jesus Laughing" images]

This Psalm of David says that the Lord laughs at the wicked and their deeds. It would seem to me that He would be angry at them - and I believe He does get angry. However, the Lord knows that it is futile to fight against Him or His children. The idea that He laughs indicates that He is not worried or sitting in heaven anxiously wringing His hands. So, how should we react when it "seems like" the wicked are attacking us?

51. GOD IS LIGHT

"This is the message we have heard from him and declare to you: God is light; in Him there is no darkness at all."   1 John 1:5 NIV

It seems that in today's age, people are more interested in death and darkness. Many movies and TV shows are about zombies (walking dead), killing, the supernatural, the dark side, etc. I have also noticed an increased interest in what people call "the day of the dead". And, today just happens to be Halloween. Many children and adults will dress up in a myriad of scary or funny costumes. It's a tradition.

However, as Christians - believers - our focus should be on the LORD our GOD in whom there is LIFE. There is no darkness in HIM because HE IS LIGHT, and HE is the "Light of the world". Our world needs to see the Light so that darkness will be exposed for what it is. Let us walk in the Light and have fellowship with our God. Celebrate the "Day of the Living"!

52. SAVOR EVERY MINUTE OF YOUR LIFE

"LORD, let me know my [life's] end And [to appreciate] the extent of my days; Let me know how frail I am [how transient is my stay here]." Psalm 39:4 AMPLIFIED

I think that most people want to live and not die. Their desire is to live and live long. The problem is that we never know how long we will be on this earth. Some people go to great lengths to enhance their health just to discover the end of their days is nearer that they thought. Vitamin and supplement companies are abundant and thriving. Gyms and fitness centers abound everywhere. People want to live long.

The only way we can find peace of mind or reconcile the question regarding the length of our life, is to go to the "Giver of Life". Ask the Lord to help us appreciate each day we wake up and every breath we take. Ask God to help us realize how short life really is and to help us savor every moment. Make the best of every given day - you never know how many you have left.

53. TOO MUCH TO TELL

"Many, Lord my God, are the wonders you have done, the things you planned for us. None can compare with you; were I to speak and tell of your deeds, they would be too many to declare."   Psalm 40:5 NIV

Have you ever been asked to say a few words in front of a group of people - at a gathering, in a class, or maybe at church? A common response is, "I don't know what to say" or "I have nothing to say". Well, when you think of God and all the things He has done, you should never be at a loss for words.

David, the Psalmist, said that if he were to speak of all the great and wonderful things that God has done, there would be too many stories (true stories) to tell. David could have spoken about God many times a day for the rest of his life. How about you? If you really have a relationship with God, you can never say you have nothing to talk about. If you are stumped when asked to speak, just recall all that God has done - then you could speak forever.

54. PUT YOUR HOPE IN GOD

"Why, my soul, are you downcast? Why so disturbed within me? Put your hope in God, for I will yet praise him, my Savior and my God." Psalm 42:11 NIV

Have you ever experienced a day when you just felt depressed? Maybe you weren't sure why, you couldn't quite figure it out. Or, maybe some failure, or sin haunted you - or maybe you were worrying about the outcome of a circumstance. I think most of us have been there. That same feeling is what I pictured when I read today's Psalm.

In the very last verse of Psalm 42, the writer asks himself some important questions - he speaks to his own soul. Why, why, he asks. Then, here's an important part for us to reflect on and remember, he SPEAKS TO himself (no, he wasn't crazy) and he tells himself to put HOPE in God. This word "hope" carries the sense of hopeful expectation - not wishful thinking. Sometimes we, like this writer, need to speak to ourselves and encourage ourselves to TRUST CONFIDENTLY IN GOD - and not let our thinking depress us.

55. LIVE WISELY BY LISTENING ATTENTIVELY
"My son, be attentive to my wisdom [godly wisdom learned by costly experience], Incline your ear to my understanding; That you may exercise discrimination and discretion (good judgment), And your lips may reserve knowledge and answer wisely [to temptation]."
Proverbs 5:1-2 AMPLIFIED BIBLE

The Amplified Bible, to me, helps illuminate the principles found in these two verses. The first admonition to the reader is to "be attentive to" or "pay close attention to" the writer's wisdom and understanding.

There is something I learned from my Dad, and I tried to pass on to my son - and that is, when you have a job, always try to find some of the older people who have been working their job for many years. Then, hang around that person, or people, and "pick their brain". Find out what they have learned and listen closely. You will gain much from their experience.

Why would this "exercise" be so valuable? So that we would learn and practice discrimination (making wise judgments) and discretion (acting properly according to those judgements). And, after learning these principles, you will be able to pass them on to the younger ones who come along behind you.

56. WHAT IS YOUR WEAPON OF CHOICE?
"I put no trust in my bow, my sword does not bring me victory; but you give us victory over our enemies, you put our adversaries to shame." Psalm 44:6-7 NIV

I have only fired a weapon a few times in my life. I received some basic training in the military (Navy), in the handling and firing of a few weapons. I also learned how to shoot a shotgun - on a Trap & Skeet range. However, I have never had to rely on weapons for survival.

We can assume that the writer of this Psalm had a lot of experience in the use of a sword and a bow. And, it appears that he had used these weapons in warfare. However, he states that he did not put full trust or confidence in these weapons for ultimate victory over his enemies. His trust was totally in the Lord to give victory over his adversaries.

What "weapons" do we put our trust in for survival - our wealth, our education, our skills, our strength, our determination, our friends, etc.? Put your trust in the Lord - only and always.

57. AVOID THE SNARE OF IMMORALITY
"My son, keep my words and store up my commands within you. Keep my commands and you will live; guard my teachings as the apple of your eye." Proverbs 7:1-2 NIV

The entirety of this Proverb is dedicated to warning young men (and may I include middle-aged and older men) about the dangers of being enticed (seduced) by immoral women. If you read the history of the author of this Proverb - Solomon - you will find that he had a lot of experience in the struggle with immorality.

The battle with immorality is real - for both men and women, young and old. And many lives have been adversely affected by poor choices. However, there is help for all. The words and commands of the Lord are not intended to make our lives miserable and tormented - they are to give us real and fulfilled life. So, learn, keep, cherish, and obey God's instructions - then you will really live and avoid the deadly snares of sin.

58. THE VOICE OF WISDOM SPEAKS

"Blessed are those who listen to me, watching daily at my doors, waiting at my doorway. For those who find me find life and receive favor from the Lord."   Proverbs 8:34-35 NIV

I remember as a young child, on Christmas Eve, eagerly waiting and watching at the sliding glass door for our Dad to get home. From this vantage point we could see the main road. Dad mostly worked evenings, and our family had a tradition of opening one present on Christmas Eve . . .when our Dad arrived home. We would start getting anxious around 11 p.m. and would start gathering by this big window to see if we could get a glimpse of him driving down the road. Sometimes we would wait for hours - but we didn't get tired.

I thought of my feelings of anticipation as I read this Proverb today. It's to those who listen, who watch, and who wait for Wisdom that life and favor are given. We shouldn't assume, or take for granted, that Wisdom will just fall into our lap. I also thought of the man written about in Psalm 1 who delighted in God's Law and meditated on it day and night. Let's learn to commit ourselves to learning Wisdom - it takes some effort and concentrated listening.

59. THUNDEROUS APPLAUSE

"Clap your hands, all you nations; shout to God with cries of joy. For the Lord Most High is awesome, the great King over all the earth."
Psalm 47:1-2 NIV

There are many scenarios that would cause people to break out in jubilant applause and shouting: sporting events, concerts, rallies, etc. And, I think many of us have been involved in one or more of these events at one time or another - so we are familiar with the experience.

In the scenarios I just mentioned, people don't have to be told to clap and shout - it seems to happen spontaneously. The feeling is also infectious. The more people applaud, others begin as well. The resounding cheers seem to cause others to try and out-shout those around them.

The Lord our God, the Awesome One, the Great King and Creator, deserves our loudest praise. SHOUT to the Lord Praises due to Him. CLAP your hands, giving Him a thunderous applause for all HE has done!

60. FOLLOW ORDERS

"The wise in heart accept commands, but a chattering fool comes to ruin."   Proverbs 10:8 NIV

The idea of accepting commands stems from recognizing authority. Foolish people do not recognize or understand the concept of authority, and they invite problems for themselves.

When I was a young man in the Navy, our ship had a collision with a other ship. We were out at sea in rough conditions, taking on ammunition from another ship. Our ships were side-by-side, and because of the heavy waves, they collided. At the time, I was unaware of the situation. There was an announcement over the ship's radio to "man your battle stations". I thought this was another "practice drill" so I just stayed in my compartment, ignoring the command to get to my station. When I was made aware that we had a collision with an ammunition-carrying ship, and that our ships were stuck together - on the same side that my compartment was on - and that there could be a disaster, I decided to obey the order to evacuate my compartment. I was being foolish and unwise. It could have turned out much worse. Bottom line - FOLLOW ORDERS!

61. WHO CAN PAY THE PRICE?

"No one can redeem the life of another or give to God a ransom for them— the ransom for a life is costly, no payment is ever enough— so that they should live on forever and not see decay."
Psalm 49:7-9 NIV

Some people state that they would lay down their life for another person - their child, their spouse, or a good friend. That might be true, and they are probably sincere, however, it would never be enough to secure eternal life for them. The Psalmist says that the cost of a life is great, too great for mere man to redeem. Does this mean that any sacrifice is in vain?

Hope for eternal life does not end here - this is not the end of the story. It is important that we don't stop here because there is an answer - a solution. The solution is "A REDEEMER", One who is worth more than the life of another person. In fact, His worth is far more valuable than all who ever lived, and who ever will live on this earth. Who Is This "REDEEMER"? Who Is This One Who's Value is Above All Others? Who is This Great One? Tell me if you know!

His Name is JESUS! He came to redeem mankind - and He paid the ultimate price that no one could ever pay. Are we worthy to be redeemed? No! But He gave His Life for us out of His LOVE. How Valuable is that?

62. THE SACRIFICE OF THANKFULNESS

"Those who sacrifice thank offerings honor me, and to the blameless I will show my salvation." Psalm 50:23 NIV

Have you ever tried to show someone how much you love and appreciate them by showing them with gifts - expensive gifts? Have you ever tried that with God - offering Him your time, dedication, or monetary offerings? This Psalm, in the previous verses, mentions giving sacrifices of burnt offerings of bulls and goats. But God asks, "Do I eat the flesh of bulls or drink the blood of goats?" God doesn't NEED your stuff, and you can't buy His favor or affection.

One thing this Psalm reveals is that offering the sacrifice of thankfulness to God actually honors Him more than offering Him all the material things in the world. Take some quality time to just THANK God for life, another breath, another day, or for the privilege of even having a conversation with Him.

"THANK YOU, LORD, our GOD, our CREATOR, our SAVIOR and GIVER OF LIFE."

63. CHECK YOUR HEART

"Have mercy on me, O God, according to your unfailing love; according to your great compassion blot out my transgressions. Wash away all my iniquity and cleanse me from my sin."
Psalm 51:1-2 NIV

Mistakes are made often. Poor decisions are made frequently. I think it is safe to say that all who read this can identify with these comments. However, in the case of King David, who wrote Psalm 51, to say a little "mistake" or a "poor decision" had been made would be a gross misunderstanding of what he had done. To put it bluntly, David misused his authority as the king, committed adultery with one of his soldier's wife, and then had that soldier killed (pre-meditated murder). This was no "small sin".

As we think of this story in Biblical history, and compare it to our lives, we may not be in the same category. But, in any case, sin is sin. As the story of King David goes, he was called-out (exposed) by Nathan the prophet, he acknowledged his sin before God, and asked for forgiveness. Why would - why should - God forgive David? Why should he forgive any of us? The "key" is found in verse 17 of Psalm 51: *"My sacrifice, O God, is a broken spirit; a broken and contrite heart you, God, will not despise."*

IT'S A HEART MATTER - Do you, do we, have a heart after God - a contrite heart? Or, is our heart hardened when sin is exposed?

64. FEAR CAN BE A FOUNTAIN OF LIFE
"The fear of the Lord is a fountain of life, turning a person from the snares of death." Proverbs 14:27 NIV

When the word "fear" is used we usually get a negative picture in our mind. Fear can cause anxiety and a rejection of that which is feared. Don't some people tend to avoid things that they are afraid of (flying, heights, public speaking, the ocean, etc.)?

However, we are told in this Proverb that the fear of the Lord is something totally different. It is not a "turning away from" or avoiding the Lord, but a respectful "trusting in" Him. Our confidence in His love for us is a "fountain", a "spring" of LIFE, which actually draws us near. Because of this "deep respectful trust", the only thing we avoid is the "snares" or "traps" of sin - which leads only to destruction and death. Do you have a healthy fear of the Lord?

65. YOU ARE WHAT YOU EAT

"The discerning heart seeks knowledge, but the mouth of a fool feeds on folly."   Proverbs 15:14 NIV

People today are so opinionated. This is partly true due to the things they see or read on social media. Not everything we read on Facebook or Twitter, or on the Internet in general, is completely factual.

There's an old adage that goes something like this: "You are what you eat." Have you heard it? Well, the meaning of that saying was written long ago, in Proverbs 15. People who are discerning (having good judgment) we're not born that way - but they search out what is true and factual. However, foolish people feed on whatever catches their attention on the News, on social media, or from friends & acquaintances.

Bottom line - don't form an inaccurate opinion or pass on inaccurate news before spending a little time checking the facts. You Are What You Eat - either Discerning or Foolish.

66. ACTION AND REACTION

"Let evil recoil on those who slander me; in your faithfulness destroy them."   Psalm 54:5 NIV

In what we refer to as "The Lord's Prayer", Jesus taught that we should forgive others as we have been forgiven. Forgiveness is a purposeful act on our part. We should allow room for God to act on our behalf (He does a much better job than we do). In this Psalm, David is praying that whatever evil others have done against him would recoil back on them.

The first thing that came to mind when I read this verse is the action experienced when shooting a hand gun or rifle . . . you know, the "kick back". And most of us remember Newton's third Law of Motion: For every action, there is an equal and opposite reaction. Well, we don't need to worry about getting back at others - Newton and David discovered the secret of one of God's principles. God will "pay back" the evil that is done to us. So, let evil RECOIL back onto the one delivering it.

67. TRANSFERRING OUR CARES TO THE ONE WHO CARES
"Cast your cares on the Lord and he will sustain you; he will never let the righteous be shaken." Psalm 55:22 NIV

Earlier this year I discovered a plumbing problem under our house - a leak in a sewer pipe. I know how difficult and expensive plumbing problems can be, and I was already thinking about "dollar signs". I knew I shouldn't put-off getting the repairs done, but I was starting to "sweat it" (worry a little).

My son had been working on a project in his garage and we were talking about the things he had to get done. I just happened to mention my plumbing problem to him. He casually said, "we could fix it EASILY". In my mind, it was no easy fix. However, my "big problem" was transferred to my son's confidence that this was a "little problem" that we could take care of easily and inexpensively. My huge "mountain" turned out to be "a piece of cake" because I turned over my problem to my son. The leak was repaired - and only a few dollars were spent.

This is how the Lord can handle the "cares" of our life - if we would only trust, I repeat, TRUST in Him.

68. IS WEALTH TRUSTWORTHY?

"The wealth of the rich is their fortified city; they imagine it a wall too high to scale." Proverbs 18:11 NIV

What is your "security blanket"? Is it your wealth? This Proverb says that those who are rich place so much trust in their money, stocks, and other assets that they actually think they will always be financially secure.

Being "rich" is relative, not absolute. In other words, we can be considered rich when compared to those who are somewhat poor. However, at the same time, we can be viewed as poor when compared to the extremely wealthy. Whatever your financial position or status, the thing, or things, you place complete confidence in will determine the condition of your heart.

Riches - money, possessions, and other assets - will ultimately perish. So, put your trust and confidence in the Eternal, Everlasting God. He never diminishes.

69. TWO PATHS

"Listen to advice and accept discipline, and at the end you will be counted among the wise." Proverbs 19:20 NIV

"Stop listening to instruction, my son, and you will stray from the words of knowledge." Proverbs 19:27 NIV

The famous Yankee baseball legend, Yogi Berra, has been known for saying, "When you come to a fork in the road . . . take it." Sounds confusing, doesn't it? Well, when you face a dilemma in life, and you're not sure which way to turn, it's always important to seek good advice and Godly Wisdom. However, some will listen, and some won't.

The writer of this Proverb gives two scenarios - two paths - in which to take: listening to advice or or not listening. Both paths have destinations with opposing results - wisdom or straying away from wisdom. Which will you choose?

70. THE LITTLE THINGS
"Ears that hear and eyes that see— the Lord has made them both."
Proverbs 20:12 NIV

Thanksgiving will be upon us in the next few days. What an interesting word "thanksgiving" is. Many people only associate this word with a holiday. However, this word actually means what it says - "giving of thanks" or being grateful. Many times, we give thanks when something awesome happens, or when someone does something for us. But what about the little things in our life?

Proverbs 20:12 identifies two little things - but important things: ears and eyes. How many times do we take for granted these parts of our body? Daily? Our ears and our eyes help us to function each and every day. Could we live effectively without them? Yes - just ask those that are deaf and blind. Sometimes, I think they are more thankful than people who can hear and see because they realize the value of those two "little" things. Let us truly be thankful for all the Lord has given us - every day, not just on Thanksgiving Day.

71. GUARD YOUR WORDS
"Those who guard their mouths and their tongues keep themselves from calamity." Proverbs 21:23 NIV

I'm sure you have said things you wish could be taken back. I know I have. Once your words leave your mouth (or your computer, phone, etc.) they are impossible to retract. On the other hand, there are times when I have said words that I just don't remember saying, but someone else does, and they bring it to my attention.

How do we handle it, or react, when someone tells us we have spoken damaging, forgotten, or untrue words? It's usually a very uncomfortable experience. But, humbly ask for forgiveness and quickly seek to clarify or amend the situation.

Therefore, let's learn to practice the instructions of this Proverb: "guard your mouth and tongue". Put a mental sentry around your mouth (or brain) to examine your words and thoughts before they are dispatched. Another helpful hint is to tell a trusted friend to review your words - ask them what they think. In doing this, you will avoid much disaster.

72. TRUST GOD FIRST
"Give us aid against the enemy, for human help is worthless. With God we will gain the victory, and he will trample down our enemies."
Psalm 60:11-12 NIV

In 2 Samuel, chapter 8, we read of many victories that King David had won. We are told that it wasn't because of the size of David's army, or His power, or his military intelligence that gave him the advantage over his enemies. No, it was the Lord who gave David victory wherever he went.

How often do we turn to human help when we are faced with difficult circumstances or major challenges in our life? The possible reason is that there is an abundance of resources available for us to turn to. But, when we run out of those resources we are forced to turn to God. Here's a great idea - let's turn to God first! Let's learn to trust in the One who is able to defeat our "enemies" and give us victory over all of life's problems.

73. SAFE PLACE

"I long to dwell in your tent forever and take refuge in the shelter of your wings." Psalm 61:4 NIV

While reading this Psalm of David this morning, I thought, "Where is my safe place?" Many people have a place where they feel totally safe and protected from all harm. For some, that place is their home or their room. Others feel like there is a spot in the mountains or at a beach where they can "get away" from all their problems and cares. Where is your "safe place"?

David wrote that he longed to dwell in the tent of the Lord. This is not an actual physical location, but it is a "place or realm" where the presence of the Lord is. And, taking refuge in a shelter speaks of a place of total safety. Is it possible for us to find that "special place" with the Lord where we feel totally protected and comforted, knowing we are in His presence? YES, WE CAN.

Let's sincerely desire to find that place close to God, experiencing His arms around us - safe and secure.

74. WHO IS YOUR "ROCK"?

"Truly my soul finds rest in God; my salvation comes from him. Truly he is my rock and my salvation; he is my fortress, I will never be shaken." Psalm 62:1-2 NIV

I think - I could be wrong - that most of us have had a time in our life when our faith has been shaken. Maybe it was more than once. Our faith could have been in others, in possessions, in our wealth, or in God - but it was tested.

In this Psalm, David wrote about his "rock", his "fortress", his stability, being in his God. This stability allowed his soul to be at rest, at peace, regardless of the circumstances. We can learn a lot from David because he wrote from his personal experiences. Let me ask this question, because we never know when our faith will be tested next: Is the Lord your God your ROCK and FORTRESS? Or will you trust in other things or people to support you?

75. CLING TO THE LORD
"Because you are my help, I sing in the shadow of your wings. I cling to you; your right hand upholds me." Psalm 63:7-8 NIV

King David wrote this Psalm/song while he was in the dry and parched desert of Judah. In the first verse, David used the terms "thirst" and "long for" indicating how desperate he was for the Lord.

I saw a picture some time ago that had a small cat hanging onto a rope with a knot at the end. It was desperately hanging on with one paw barely attached. There was a caption at the bottom of the picture that said, "When You Come to the End of Your Rope, Tie a Knot And Hang On!" That's the image that came to my mind when I read Psalm 63 - especially in verse 8 where David said, "I cling to" the Lord. And I picture the Lord's right hand like a knot at the end of a rope. THE LORD IS OUR HELP - SO, DON'T REFUSE GOD'S HAND. HANG ON!

76. POUR OUT YOUR HEART TO GOD

"Hear me, my God, as I voice my complaint; protect my life from the threat of the enemy. Hide me from the conspiracy of the wicked, from the plots of evildoers."   Psalm 64:1-2 NIV

David's prayer, or "complaint" (as some translations use this word) against his enemies' "threats" is difficult to fully understand unless we first acquaint ourselves with David's life. The threats and conspiracies that David referred to were not just simple plans to make him miserable or ruin his reputation. No, they were actual plans by those who hated and feared David, to kill him.

Our life's situations seem so trivial when we compare them to what David faced. We don't like to "complain" or whine to God . . . do we? However, we should feel just as comfortable to pour out our hearts to God as David did. When we do express ourselves to God like David did, it demonstrates that we trust Him and are confident that He will help us. Go ahead and complain to God. Pour out your heart to Him. He loves to hear from us.

77. OTHERS SEE WHAT YOU DON'T SEE

"As water reflects the face, so one's life reflects the heart."
Proverbs 27:19 NIV

"Reflect" means to cast back at or throw back at. Our face tells a story, it emits what's going on inside - and we can't see that story unless we look in a mirror. Our reflection in water or a mirror reveals back to us what others see firsthand. When others see our face, they see a "story" going on. Many times, we wear a mask to hide the true story.

However, the way we live, or our daily conduct, reveals much more - it shows the true condition of our heart. It is very difficult to "mask" an ungodly heart. "Lord, create in us a clean/pure heart so others can see Your reflection in us."

78. SMILEY FACE

"May God be gracious to us and bless us and make his face shine on us— so that your ways may be known on earth, your salvation among all nations."   Psalm 67:1-2 NIV

The idea of the Lord's face "shining on us" intrigued me. What came to mind was how we feel relieved when someone smiles at us verses when they frown at us. Just that little facial expression tells us a lot. It's the difference between light and darkness. I don't recall too many times when I received a smile from my Dad, but I sure remember the frowns. Isn't it strange that at my age I still remember that?

A smile is something that we can give and receive, and it doesn't cost anything - but, oh how valuable it can be. And to think of God Almighty smiling at you, and at me, is something to be treasured. To imagine His "face shining" on us, to me, is to see a huge grin on His face, from ear to ear. What a thing to treasure! God's great love and grace is to be cherished, and it causes us to want to share that with others.

79. BURDEN BEARER

"Praise be to the Lord, to God our Savior, who daily bears our burdens." Psalm 68:19 NIV

Do you have problems or challenges in your life? I know that many people do have them, and they carry around a heavy load. That's being responsible, right? It is good to take responsibility for our own life and not blame everything and everyone for our situations.

However, if we know God, our Lord and Savior, in a personal way, we can trust that He is not only with us, but He also helps us. In Psalm 68 we read that the Lord bears our daily burdens. Jesus, in Matthew 11:28-

30, personally invites us to come to Him if we are tired and have heavy burdens - and He will give us rest. So, don't try to carry more than you can handle. Take a load off and sit down with your "burden-bearer", your "care-carrier". Praise the Lord for His assistance in our life! When we are weak, He is strong.

80. THE PURPOSE OF PROVERBS

The author, Solomon, begins his writings with the purpose for his proverbs:

"for gaining wisdom and instruction; for understanding words of insight; for receiving instruction in prudent behavior, doing what is right and just and fair; for giving prudence to those who are simple, knowledge and discretion to the young . . ." Proverbs 1:2-4 NIV

Before we start undertaking the task of reading through the book of Proverbs, we are able to see the real value in doing so. These Proverbs are designed for reaching every kind of person - the educated and the uneducated, the young and the old, the weak and the strong.

These Proverbs provide us with something more valuable than all the gold and silver we could amass: Wisdom, Knowledge, Understanding, and Instruction. There is guidance in these inspired writings for our behavior, so that we might do what is right and just and fair. So, read every day, soak it all in, and live it out.

81. FAMILY DECLARATION

"Even when I am old and gray, do not forsake me, my God, till I declare your power to the next generation, your mighty acts to all who are to come." Psalm 71:18 NIV

This has been the prayer on my heart lately - not the "old and gray" part - but that I have properly declared, and will continue to declare, to my children, grandchildren, and great-grandchildren, the power of God to not only change our life for the better, but also to help us live as we ought to live. I pray that I will be an example to my family that we can place our absolute trust in God to watch over us, protect us, and help us.

I realize that I am not perfect, and I often still make mistakes, but the God I know and love and serve is GRACIOUS, full of COMPASSION and MERCY. My desire is that my family, for generations to come, will come to experience their own personal relationship with our Heavenly Father and Savior Jesus Christ. Lord, help me to make this declaration loud and clear, yet humbly and lovingly.

82. LIKE A MOTHER HEN

"Get wisdom, get understanding; do not forget my words or turn away from them. Do not forsake wisdom, and she will protect you; love her, and she will watch over you."   Proverbs 4:5-6 NIV

Wisdom, in this Proverb, is referred to as a female. However, the instructions are coming from a father to a son (see verse 1). And, the father is not making a casual suggestion - he is making a command: GET wisdom! GET understanding! DON'T forget, DON'T turn away! Sounds a bit like a Drill Sergeant to me.

Have you ever noticed a difference between a father's (male) way of teaching versus a mother's (female) way of teaching? I thought of Timothy, in the Bible, and how he was taught the Scriptures by his grandmother and his mother. WISDOM, according to Solomon, deals with us like a mother or grandmother would: lovingly watching over us and protecting us - like a "mother hen". When you view wisdom and understanding in this way, it seems easier to be attracted to it. So, let's go get it!

83. DOES GOD HOLD YOUR HAND?

"I was senseless and ignorant; I was a brute beast before You. Yet I am always with You; You hold me by my right hand. You guide me with Your counsel, and afterward You will take me into glory."
Psalm 73:22-24 NIV

I was just watching the funeral service for former President George H. W. Bush this morning. There were many, many great words spoken about this man. And, as I read Psalm 73 this morning, I stopped and reflected on verses 22-24.

The Psalmist realized that he was senseless and ignorant before God - he was far from being perfect or holy. But, he had, and he maintained, a relationship with God because he realized how much the Lord had been with him and led him through life. The people who spoke at George H. W. Bush's Funeral this morning offered similar words about the former President.

I encourage you to consider your relationship with God. Do you recognize Him and His counsel in every part of your life? Is He leading you and guiding you? Are you following Him?

84. PICNIC SPOILER OR EXAMPLE TO FOLLOW?

"Go to the ant, you sluggard; consider its ways and be wise! It has no commander, no overseer or ruler, yet it stores its provisions in summer and gathers its food at harvest."   Proverbs 6:6-8 NIV

"Sluggards" are lazy people. In this Proverb, Solomon advises sluggards to look closely at how ants behave. Solomon must have spent some time observing ants because he points out some of their interesting behaviors. He says that even though they have no leaders, they perform individually, on their own and yet in unison with other ants, like a well-oiled machine. The ants form large colonies with each kind of ant (queen, drone, soldier, or worker) performing perfectly without any direction. They instinctively know what they are supposed to do.

Ant colonies are described as 'superorganisms' because the ants appear to operate as a unified entity, collectively working together to support the colony. Wouldn't it be great to see things work so well in the environments we are familiar with (at home, or our jobs, the government, or even in our churches)? Wherever you are, don't be lazy. Don't wait to be told what to do. Look around for something that needs attention and take care of it. Work in harmony with others. CONSIDER THE ANT.

85. SAFEKEEPING OF GOD'S WORD
"My son, keep my words and store up my commands within you."
Proverbs 7:1 NIV

"I have hidden your word in my heart that I might not sin against you."
Psalm 119:11 NIV

Some people rent Safe Deposit Boxes at their local banks to keep their valuables in for safekeeping. They consider these "valuables" so precious and important that they don't want them stolen or misplaced. Both Solomon and David regarded God's Word as being this valuable - valuable enough for safekeeping.

So, how do we "store up" or "hide" the Word of God? Or, do we even count the Word of God as being of great value? If we do, the way to to properly handle God's Word is to read it often, research its meaning in proper context, memorize it, and meditate on it over and over. This process will engraft the Word in our heart. As a result, it will shape and mold our lives into Christlikeness.

86. WISDOM ADVERTISED

"Does not wisdom call out? Does not understanding raise her voice? At the highest point along the way, where the paths meet, she takes her stand;"   Proverbs 8:1-2 NIV

Wisdom is not esoteric or arcane (known only to a select few). It is not mysterious or hidden. Proverbs 8 tells us that wisdom is open and exposed - making itself readily available to all. It stands out like the biggest billboard you've ever seen along a freeway, advertising its great value.

Advertisements are designed to "catch" people's attention, hoping to get a positive response - and this is exactly what Solomon is writing here. Wisdom cries out: "DON'T PASS IT UP - DON'T MISS IT! I'M AVAILABLE . . . FREE!" Why then, are there so many unwise people (even "believers") making unwise choices? Get Wisdom, Godly Wisdom - Pursue Understanding with all diligence. You won't be disappointed.

87. REMEMBER TO REMEMBER

The writer of Psalm 77 was in a state of despair when he wrote these words:
"Then I thought, 'To this I will appeal: the years when the Most High stretched out his right hand. I will remember the deeds of the Lord; yes, I will remember your miracles of long ago. I will consider all your works and meditate on all your mighty deeds.'"   Psalm 77:10-12 NIV

Our lives don't always go as planned, or as we might expect. This might cause us to wonder where God is, or doubt if He hears us, or question if He is aware of our situation. We should know better - but sometimes we need to remind ourselves of how God has taken care of us, and others. Then, there are times when we need others to remind us.

The Bible is a great resource for testimonies of God's care and protection and miracles. And, the testimonies of other people are also encouraging. However, there are times when we just need to remind ourselves to consider (meditate on) all the ways God has "shown up" when we needed Him the most.

88. WHAT ARE YOU LOOKING FOR?
"Whoever seeks good finds favor, but evil comes to one who searches for it." Proverbs 11:27 NIV

Isn't it interesting that when we lose something we usually search and search feverishly to find it - especially if it's something valuable or important? Recently, a friend of mine misplaced a check and spent a lot of time searching for it until they finally found it. How many of us will exercise the same diligence and persistence to seek out the good things of life?

Evil and negativity is abundant, and you can always find it almost everywhere. It doesn't take much effort to discover something wrong or negative with a situation or with other people. But, it's more productive and beneficial when we, like Indiana Jones looking for the lost ark, exert our energy and our time looking for the good things of life and in people as often as we can. Determine to be a "prospector of the positive" or "spelunker of the superb".

89. DON'T THINK YOU ARE ALWAYS RIGHT
"The way of fools seems right to them, but the wise listen to advice."
Proverbs 12:15 NIV

I have heard it said that belly buttons and opinions are alike - everybody has one. Almost everyone thinks they are right in the way they feel about something or someone, or how things are meant to be. That's the way we operate. This Proverb, though, states that fools believe their way is always right.

Let me let you in on a secret - you are not always correct in your thinking. When new evidence or facts are introduced to us, our opinions can change - unless we are blind or just plain stubborn. Solomon tells us in this Proverb that wise people will listen to advice - they are open to changing the way they think. This actually happened to me while I was on Jury Duty recently. Don't fear being wrong - always ask for advice from those who have proven to be wise.

90. REPAYMENT OR REWARD - WHICH WOULD YOU PREFER?
"I am the Lord your God, who brought you up out of Egypt. Open wide your mouth and I will fill it. "But my people would not listen to me; Israel would not submit to me. So I gave them over to their stubborn hearts to follow their own devices."   Psalm 81:10-12 NIV

"The faithless will be fully repaid for their ways, and the good rewarded for theirs."   Proverbs 14:14 NIV

Have you ever tried to tell someone else's child to behave and they boldly look you right in the face and say, "You can't tell me what to do!" Have you ever had this happen with your own children? It's far more serious when your children disrespect you or rebel against you. This is the idea mentioned in Psalm 81. God's people wouldn't listen to Him because of their stubbornness (hard heart). It wasn't some other nation or people - it was Israel.

The resulting action from God was to give them what their hearts desired. You might think this was "bad parenting" but God is both wise and just. He knew the results of Israel's rebellion - as He does our rebellious ways - and this is not what He desires for us. Then, in Proverbs 14 we read that God "repaid" the faithless (reap what they sow), but He REWARDS those who are good and obedient. Would you rather rebel and get repaid, or obey and get rewarded?

91. BE WISE AND FEAR GOD
"Wisdom's instruction is to fear the Lord, and humility comes before honor." Proverbs 15:33 NIV

There's an old Country song by Mac Davis that goes like this:
"Oh Lord it's hard to be humble when you're perfect in every way.
I can't wait to look in the mirror
Cause I get better looking each day".

There may be people who think like that, but they will find it difficult to fear God or to humble themselves before God or others. And here's a nugget of wisdom for you: Humility - being humble - will keep you from being Humiliated. So, bow before the King of Glory, the LORD, and cast all of your crowns at His feet. God doesn't care how good looking you are or how much you have accomplished or how many riches you have amassed for yourself. But He does want your heart.

92. SAFE DRIVING
"The highway of the upright avoids evil; those who guard their ways preserve their lives." Proverbs 16:17 NIV

I was just thinking about some of the people I saw on the news recently who tried driving their cars through flooded streets. Some of the areas in Southern California had experienced devastating fires, and a few weeks later, heavy rains. The rains caused some flooding and mud slides. When some local roads were being washed out, there were a few people that tried to drive down the roads. The water didn't appear to be too deep, so they gave it a try anyway. You guessed it - they got stuck. And some even had to be rescued before they drowned inside their car.

Proverbs 16:17 speaks of a highway. The "upright" travel on a good, safe highway, avoiding evil and danger. They guard their way and guard their life. Therefore, if you want to keep safe, don't take dangerous chances. Guard your way, watch for "potholes" and "pitfalls" along your path, and avoid them. Set "guardrails" along your life's highway to avoid the dangers of evil. Stay UPRIGHT, my friend!

93. NEARNESS TO GOD

"How lovely is your dwelling place, Lord Almighty! My soul yearns, even faints, for the courts of the Lord; my heart and my flesh cry out for the living God."   Psalm 84:1-2 NIV

"Better is one day in your courts than a thousand elsewhere; I would rather be a doorkeeper in the house of my God than dwell in the tents of the wicked."   Psalm 84:10 NIV

We sing parts of this Psalm in our church. It's a great song. But even greater is the meaning contained within these words. The Psalmist writes about how lovely the dwelling place of the Lord is to Him. There is almost a desperate longing sensed in this writing just to be near the Lord. The words "dwelling place" and "courts" indicate being in the vicinity of God, and I can almost feel the writer's persistent desire to get as close as possible.

Here's a challenge to all of us: Take a good look at how strong our desire is for God's presence and for our "closeness" to Him. And, check this out . . . even if we were not able to get as close as we desire, or as close as we might think we deserve, would we be OK if we were only a "doorkeeper" in God's house - letting others go in and out while we stay at our post?

94. FAITHFULNESS IS OPPOSITE OF FOOLISHNESS
"I will listen to what God the Lord says; he promises peace to his people, his faithful servants— but let them not turn to folly. Surely his salvation is near those who fear him, that his glory may dwell in our land." Psalm 85:8-9 NIV

God's promises are certain. They can be fully counted on and trusted. This Psalmist writes about listening to the Lord's promises of peace to "His people". Is everyone classified as "His people"? Well, there is clarification in this verse: "His faithful servants". God's promise of peace is to those who are faithful to God.

Faithfulness is the opposite of foolishness - and God's people are not to be given to folly, or foolishness. Surely, our fear of God (a mixture of deep respect and fearfulness) keeps us faithful, keeps us near to God, and gives us the peace of His salvation. This is what God promises - listen to Him.

95. ARE YOU BLAMING GOD?
"A person's own folly leads to their ruin, yet their heart rages against the Lord." Proverbs 19:3 NIV

Have you ever been mad at God? I know I have. Think back for a moment - what caused you to become angry? Was it because He didn't answer your prayer, or that something bad happened to you, or to someone you loved? Now, ask yourself this question: "How would I have answered my prayer, or changed my situation?" Better yet, examine your involvement - what were you doing, how were you acting, what were your motives?

Many times, we are the cause of our own predicaments. Let's face it - we are sometimes foolish in our thinking, our desires, and our actions. We struggle at times with our "old nature" - our "flesh". Then, we refuse to take responsibility, so we blame others or, as Solomon wrote, our *heart rages against the Lord*. We blame God for not intervening in what we have caused. Therefore, consider your ways, take responsibility for your involvement in your circumstances, and quit blaming God.

If this message is not for you, pass it on to someone else.

96. THINK BEFORE YOU SPEAK
"It is a trap to dedicate something rashly and only later to consider one's vows."   Proverbs 20:25 NIV

In Judges 11:30, Jephthah made a vow/promise to the Lord that if the Lord would give the Ammonites into his hand, he would sacrifice the first thing that came out of the door of his home as a burnt offering. To his surprise, his own daughter was the first to come out to meet him. Oops! Do you think Jephthah asked for a "do over"? Have you ever promised the Lord, or someone else, that you would surely do something if . . . (insert your own comment here)? That's called a conditional promise: "I will, if you do". Many times, we can't, or don't want to keep our end of the deal - even when we get what we desire.

Consider carefully what you are vowing to do before you open your mouth, especially when promising the Lord something. In many cases, it may be better not to make a vow at all.

97. UNPLOWED FIELDS PRODUCE WEEDS OF SIN
"Haughty eyes and a proud heart— the unplowed field of the wicked— produce sin." Proverbs 21:4 NIV

An arrogant, snobbish look on a person's face reveals something deeper within that person's heart. It reminds me, as this Proverb states, of an unplowed field - or a vacant lot overgrown with weeds. Question: where do all these weeds come from? I'm sure nobody sneaks in and plants them - and then waters the lot. They actually come from the unplowed roots lying underground that have never been completely removed.

This is what the writer of Proverbs is revealing about sin in one's life - in one who is considered "wicked". These are the ones who neglect the condition of their heart. Don't let your heart go unexamined. Let God break up the ground of your heart through prayer and reading His Word. When any root of sin (weeds) is revealed, quickly deal with that root - and remove it.

98. EVEN IF WE DON'T PRAISE, THE HEAVENS WILL
"I will sing of the Lord's great love forever; with my mouth I will make your faithfulness known through all generations." Psalm 89:1 NIV

"The heavens praise your wonders, Lord, your faithfulness too, in the assembly of the holy ones." Psalm 89:5 NIV

This Psalm-writer, Ethan the Ezrahite, expresses that he will sing with his mouth to let others (all generations) know of God's love and faithfulness. It appears that he had already made up his mind that he was going to sing, no matter what happens in his life. Can we say that?

Will we sing about the Lord's great love and His wonders - in the good times and in the bad?

Another important thing Ethan brings to our attention is that even if we don't give God praise, even if we don't tell others of HIS greatness and faithfulness, <u>THE HEAVENS WILL!</u> So, we might as well sing along: *"Holy, Holy, Holy, is the Lord God Almighty!"*

99. MONEY FLIES
"Do not wear yourself out to get rich; do not trust your own cleverness. Cast but a glance at riches, and they are gone, for they will surely sprout wings and fly off to the sky like an eagle."   Proverbs 23:4-5 NIV

Did you know this? I just checked. Our paper currency all has a picture of an eagle on them - it's on the United States Federal Reserve Seal. When I read today's Proverb about riches sprouting wings and flying off like an eagle, I just had to take a look at some of the bills I had left - the ones that haven't flown away yet.

There's a lot of financial wisdom in these verses. We shouldn't overwork ourselves just to make more money - because we will only spend more of that hard-earned money. And when it is spent, it's spent. It's gone. Then, we get caught in a vicious cycle - downward spiral - of trying to make more money. As the writer of this Proverb says, "do not trust in your own cleverness" or, as another version says, "Have the wisdom to show restraint."

100. FINDING REST IN GOD'S SHADOW
"Whoever dwells in the shelter of the Most High will rest in the shadow of the Almighty."   Psalm 91:1 NIV

People sometimes post funny videos on the internet showing a young child discovering their shadow for the first time. They are either terrified or intrigued by this strange "thing" following them. Shadows, or shade, can be something we actually desire.

A few years ago, I was in Baja, Cabo San Jose, and it was extremely hot. Walking in the sun was draining - even the ocean water was hot too. It was quite a relief to find some shade - the shadow of a building or a bridge. Proverbs 91 speaks of "dwelling in the shelter of" and "resting in the shadow of" Almighty God. What a place of REST for our souls, "sheltering" in the presence of God! What a RELIEF for our weariness. Have you found that Place? Are you dwelling there? Seek His Shadow.

101. SINCERE AND SPECIFIC PRAISE

"It is good to praise the Lord and make music to your name, O Most High, proclaiming your love in the morning and your faithfulness at night" Psalm 92:1-2 NIV

Praising the Lord - morning and evening - is good. But what is the best way to do that? Some Christians that I've known have a habit of saying "Praise the Lord" after every few words - you know, as "filler words". That makes it a bit insincere, in my opinion.

The psalmist is saying that proclaiming to others specifically how much God loves us, and how faithful He is to us, is the way to give proper praise. Instead of being "generic" and vague, tell people exactly what the Lord has done to demonstrate His love and faithfulness. Give your personal testimony often. Share stories of how the Lord has protected you or provided for your needs. Be specific.

102. THE LORD IS ROYALLY ROBED

"The Lord reigns, he is robed in majesty; the Lord is robed in majesty and armed with strength; indeed, the world is established, firm and secure." Psalm 93:1 NIV

What a contrast from the Christmas story - about the Christ child, Jesus, being born in a manger wrapped in cloths. Some versions of the Bible use the term "swaddling cloths" or strips of cloth similar to bandages. However, Psalm 93 states that the Lord is "robed in majesty".

I realize that it's cute to think of "baby Jesus", but that's not how we should view our Lord and Savior. He is robed as a glorious King, He is all powerful (omnipotent), and He rules the world. The major problem is that the world does not recognize or accept or obey the Lord's authority. Our God does reign, and the earth is firmly held together (established) because of Him - not forces of "nature". We should recognize God's power over all and give Him the honor due to Him.

103. A WANDERING MIND IS DANGEROUS

"Unless the Lord had given me help, I would soon have dwelt in the silence of death. When I said, "My foot is slipping," your unfailing love, Lord, supported me. When anxiety was great within me, your consolation brought me joy." Psalm 94:17-19 NIV

From Wikipedia: "Anxiety is an emotion characterized by an unpleasant state of inner turmoil, often accompanied by nervous behavior, somatic complaints, and rumination. It is the subjectively unpleasant feelings of dread over anticipated events, such as the feeling of imminent death. Anxiety is not the same as fear, which is a response to a real or perceived immediate threat, whereas anxiety involves the expectation of future threat."

Note that this definition states "a perceived threat or danger". Our imagination is powerful and can be paralyzingly detrimental to healthy living. The Psalmist writes that if it had not been for God, he might have died. The consolation of God is His Truth and His Holy Spirit given to us.

Be careful what you allow your mind to dwell on. Discipline your mind to read and meditate (ruminate) on the Truth and Comfort of God's Word. The consolation of having a relationship with "The Truth" brings joy, not inner turmoil.

104. TRUE VERSUS IMITATION

"For great is the Lord and most worthy of praise; he is to be feared above all gods. For all the gods of the nations are idols, but the Lord made the heavens." Psalm 96:4-5 NIV

The psalmist makes reference here to other "gods", the "gods" of the nations. He sets apart the Lord God, and places Him above all other "gods" and identifies them as idols. The dictionary defines an idol as: "an image or other material object representing a deity to which religious worship is addressed."

Our LORD GOD does not "represent" deity - HE is Deity. Our LORD GOD is not an "image" - HE is a reality, the Real Thing! And HE is Great and Worthy of all Praise for HE is above all things. HE is The Creator of all things. Worship Him only. Anything or anyone else is only imitation.

105. WORSHIP AT GOD'S FEET

"Exalt the Lord our God and worship at his footstool; he is holy." Psalm 99:5 NIV

A footstool is something that someone rests their feet on. We know that God never gets tired. He doesn't need rest. However, in the account of creation, God "rested" on the 7th day (Genesis 2:2). But that doesn't mean He needed a rest - a "breather". No, it means that He ceased creating because His plan for the world and universe was completed.

To "worship at His footstool" is to humble ourselves under God's authority - under His Lordship of all creation - while we realize and honor His worthiness and holiness. In Isaiah 66:1, the Lord says that the earth is His footstool. In other words, He rules and reigns over our realm. Can you imagine laying at the feet of Jesus and kissing His feet in worship? That would be repulsive to do to anyone else - But HE is HOLY. HE is WORTHY.

106. THE MOST VALUABLE ORNAMENT

"My son, do not let wisdom and understanding out of your sight, preserve sound judgment and discretion; they will be life for you, an ornament to grace your neck." Proverbs 3:21-22 NIV

The entire book of Proverbs is full of wise instructions that are beneficial and essential for healthy and prosperous living. King Solomon gives us a mental picture of a type of necklace we can wear around our neck. A weird image came to my mind when I read this. In the entertainment industry, a lot of rappers wear thick gold Hip Hop chains with huge pendants attached to them. One even has a large clock on his chain. Why?

Well, the "ornament" that Solomon was writing about is an "ornament of life" reflecting Godly Wisdom, Understanding, Sound Judgement, and Discretion - more specifically, "Godly Character". And you never have to fear someone stealing it from you. It doesn't tarnish because it is genuine (fake jewelry turns your skin green). Seek the "Real Thing" to display around your neck. Show real Life!

107. JOYFUL WORSHIP
"Shout for joy to the Lord, all the earth. Worship the Lord with gladness; come before him with joyful songs." Psalm 100:1-2 NIV

When I read this Psalm this morning, an old "spiritual song" popped into my head:
> *"Nobody knows the trouble I've seen, Nobody knows but Jesus*
> *Nobody knows the trouble I've seen, Glory, Hallelujah*
>
> *Sometimes I'm up*
> *And sometimes I'm down*
> *Yes, Lord, you know sometimes I'm almost to the ground*
> *Oh, yes, Lord, still, Nobody knows the trouble I've seen*
> *Nobody knows but Jesus"*

Though this song may truly reflect how we feel sometimes, it's not a very "Joyful" song. Sometimes, songs like this keep us down and close to the ground. But lift up your eyes - look toward heaven - see Jesus high and lifted up! Exalt Him with JOYFUL songs. Let there be GLADNESS in our singing. Let there be Thanksgiving and Praise . . . because of who HE is!

108. WHAT DOES GOD SEE?
"For your ways are in full view of the Lord, and he examines all your paths." Proverbs 5:21 NIV

Here's a sobering statement from Solomon - the Lord not only "sees" our ways, but He also "examines" them. One definition of the word "examine" is: to inspect or scrutinize carefully. There's no way we can escape the eyes of the Lord. There is no place we can hide.

71

There is a two-fold truth to the thought of God examining our ways: 1) To find fault; or 2) To find what we are doing right. My first inclination is to think He is scrutinizing every wrong thought, motive, and action. However, God is our Father. And, as a father myself, I look for what good things my children are doing. And, I believe that God also looks proudly at His children when He observes us doing something right - something that reflects His own character. What does God see when He watches you?

109. THE LORD HEARS, THE LORD SEES
"Hear my prayer, Lord; let my cry for help come to you. Do not hide your face from me when I am in distress. Turn your ear to me; when I call, answer me quickly." Psalm 102:1-2 NIV

Have you ever felt like God wasn't listening to your prayers, especially when you were in distress? When there was nobody that would or could possibly help you, you cried out to God in desperation and then . . . nothing but silence! That's what this Psalmist is writing about.

However, a sigh of relief is noticed a few verses later in this Psalm. The Lord is described by the psalmist as "looking down from heaven", or His sanctuary, to view the earth and to hear the groans of the people. Answers came. Action was taken. So, when we pray, we must be assured that the Lord does hear us, He is aware of our situation, and HE WILL RESPOND. Don't give up hope!

110. GOD'S COMPASSION IS STIRRED BY A RIGHT HEART
"The Lord is compassionate and gracious, slow to anger, abounding in love." Psalm 103:8 NIV

"As a father has compassion on his children, so the Lord has compassion on those who fear him; for he knows how we are formed, he remembers that we are dust."   Psalm 103:13-14 NIV

King David, the author of this Psalm, writes often about God's love, mercy and compassion. He had experienced these attributes of God first-hand as a result of his failures and some of his greatest sins. But it wasn't "automatic" - there was a qualifying factor in David's character. This qualifying factor was David's fear of God and his right response to God.

David had a heart after God's heart. He had a close, loving relationship with God, yet he feared the power and awesomeness of God as well. David also knew the compassion that an earthly father has for his own children. The compassion of God, and the mercy of God is set in motion when His children recognize their sin and repent out of their love and respect (fear) for their Heavenly Father. God's compassion isn't just "automatic" - it is stirred by a right heart.

111. CHOOSE YOUR INVESTMENTS WISELY
"Choose my instruction instead of silver, knowledge rather than choice gold, for wisdom is more precious than rubies, and nothing you desire can compare with her."   Proverbs 8:10-11 NIV

The stock market continually fluctuates up and down. People constantly watch for a good time to buy and sell their stocks. But when the market takes a sharp downward turn, panic sets in. Some investors rave on buying gold or silver because they are more stable and profitable. What is the wisest decision to make?

Solomon writes here in this chapter, that instead of focusing on the value of silver, gold, and precious gems (rubies), we should choose Godly instruction, knowledge, and wisdom. There is more value in these things to provide a stable, profitable and fulfilled life - and their value never fluctuates. In fact, nothing can compare with the value of Wisdom. Which will you choose?

112. TELL WHAT YOU'VE SEEN AND HEARD
"Give praise to the Lord, proclaim his name; make known among the nations what he has done." Psalm 105:1 NIV

Sometimes I like to watch shows on television that have court cases. But when it comes to me serving on Jury Duty, I cringe. I don't enjoy being involved in an actual case. However, one thing the television court cases have, as well as actual court cases, is "Testimonies". People are asked to give the court (judge, jurors, attorneys, court recorder) a true and accurate testimony - what they saw and what they heard.

Christians - people who have had a personal encounter with the Lord - are encouraged to, and even commanded to, share their testimony with others. If we know for a fact that God Loves us, and that Jesus Christ died for us, and that our sins are forgiven so we can have a relationship with the One and Only eternal, almighty God, we should, and need to, share this testimony (or "TELLamony") with everyone we can. Let's tell what God has done!

113. FIRMLY PLANTED
"When the storm has swept by, the wicked are gone, but the righteous stand firm forever." Proverbs 10:25 NIV

"The righteous will never be uprooted, but the wicked will not remain in the land." Proverbs 10:30 NIV

Every one of us have a few "storms" in our lifetime. Storms are never any fun, but they will happen. There's one thing about storms - they

74

don't last forever. Solomon writes about the storm having swept by. It seems like we have seen many storms lately: hurricanes, typhoons, heavy rains, and even fire storms. After each storm there is always something left standing - not a lot of things, but some things, the strong and stable things.

Solomon compares the "righteous" with those strong, sturdy, unshakable, unmovable things that remain when all else has been uprooted (the wicked). If we remain in God's favor and righteousness, we will stand firm - no storm can devastate us. We are firmly planted.

114. UPRIGHT OR UNFAITHFUL?
"The integrity of the upright guides them, but the unfaithful are destroyed by their duplicity."   Proverbs 11:3 NIV

There are four important words in this verse. Two of them are connected to each other and the other two are diametrically opposed to the first two. The two that are connected are "integrity" and "upright". The definition of integrity is: adherence to moral and ethical principles; sound moral and ethical character. This describes the upright person. The other two words are "unfaithful" and "duplicity".

The opposite of a person with integrity is the "unfaithful", or a person who demonstrates "duplicity" (other Bible versions use the words Perverseness, Crookedness, or Deviousness). Other common terms are "two-faced", "hypocritical", or "speaking with a forked-tongue".

Let's examine ourselves carefully and correct any attitude, speech, or behavior that might be opposed to our testimony. Hypocrites are "actors" - don't just "act like" you are a Christian . . . do your best to BE ONE!

115. CONFIDENCE IN GOD'S HELP

"Save us and help us with your right hand, that those you love may be delivered." Psalm 108:6 NIV

"Give us aid against the enemy, for human help is worthless." Psalm 108:12 NIV

There are some people who never like to ask for help. Do you know anyone like that? I remember an old commercial on television, many years ago, about some product which I can't remember, where a woman says in frustration, "Mother, PLEASE, I can do it myself!" Maybe it's an ego problem. Or, they have had too many experiences with people trying to help while failing, or by making the situation worse.

In this Psalm, David knew when to call for help and WHO to call. He was well-acquainted with God's power to save him from the enemies of his life. And though David had access to a mighty army of fighting men, he knew that they were not his ultimate source for victory. He even called "human help", or man's help, WORTHLESS.

Lord, help us learn to trust in Your help and in the power of Your right hand in every situation.

116. DISCIPLINE = LOVE

"Whoever spares the rod hates their children, but the one who loves their children is careful to discipline them." Proverbs 13:24 NIV

Discipline and Love - these two words don't quite seem to go together. The one, we despise, and the other, well, we love. Discipline is something I grew up with - my Dad was good at it. And, "sparing the rod" (belt) was rare. I can't count the number of spankings I received. Now days, people frown on spanking children.

This verse in Proverbs does not encourage "beating" children with a rod, a belt, a switch, or with a hand. However, in that day, chastising by spanking was acceptable. But, "Discipline" is not for inflicting cruel and unusual physical punishment on a person. "Discipline" is for training and correcting people to do what is right. We should discipline out of Love and not anger. Proverbs 3:12 tells us that God disciplines those He loves. Discipline shows that someone cares - someone loves.

117. FEAR IS A FOUNTAIN
"The fear of the Lord is a fountain of life, turning a person from the snares of death." Proverbs 14:27 NIV

FEAR is a powerful emotion. FEAR can cripple or empower us. Solomon writes in this Proverb that FEAR, properly focused, can be a "fountain of life". Fear of, or a deep respect for, the "Giver of Life" (God), makes real life not only full and thriving, but also a deterrent from death traps.

An excerpt from an article in Psychology Today says: "Fear is a vital response to physical and emotional danger. If people didn't feel fear, they couldn't protect themselves from legitimate threats." As interesting as this sounds, we humans have failed miserably at protecting ourselves from all of life's threats and dangers.

There is ONE true PROTECTOR - the ONE who has created us - Our God and Father. Fear, respect, and honor HIM, and you will really live.

118. WEIGH THE FACTS

"Great are the works of the Lord; they are pondered by all who delight in them." Psalm 111:2 NIV

The workings of the Lord are awesome - producing awe in those who experience them. The psalmist says that the Lord's works are "PONDERED". To ponder means to consider, meditate on, or to weigh carefully. I get a mental picture of someone carefully weighing something on a calibrated scale. An accurate measurement is important to determine the true weight or value of a substance.

When we face the many and varied challenges of life, stop and consider - meditate on - carefully weigh all the good things the Lord has done, is doing, and will continue to do. Isn't HE Awesome?

119. TRUSTING THE LORD IN TIMES OF UNCERTAINTY

"Surely the righteous will never be shaken; they will be remembered forever. They will have no fear of bad news; their hearts are steadfast, trusting in the Lord." Psalm 112:6-7 NIV

I don't think anyone enjoys hearing bad news. Bad news is unsettling, it shakes and tests our faith and confidence. Isn't it great to go from day to day hearing nothing but good news - great news? But we know from experience that bad news is bound to come our way. That's reality.

The important question is: How do we handle bad news? The Psalmist writes that the "righteous" are not shaken, they don't fall apart when their "world is rocked". Most of us know that feeling of receiving news of threat, or danger, or loss. But, who among us know the victory of steadfastly trusting in the Lord when we hear news that we don't want to hear? The "righteous" know. The Lord CAN BE TRUSTED! Have no fear - our Lord is near, and He cares for us.

120. GOD'S WATCHFUL EYE
"Who is like the Lord our God, the One who sits enthroned on high, who stoops down to look on the heavens and the earth?"
Psalm 113:5-6 NIV

Who, or what, can be compared with our God? No one, nobody, nothing, no how, no way! Even our English is incapable of properly describing HIM or what HE is like.

An earthly king, or ruler, may sit on their throne, in their palace, overseeing the territory they have authority over - but they can't see everything. They are actually very limited. But our God - the Lord and King over all - has HIS throne in the highest place, overlooking the heavens and the earth. And HE SEES ALL! We, HIS children, can never escape HIS watchful eye. Thank God that nothing escapes HIM. Aren't we Blessed?

121. TWO EARS – ONE MOUTH
Proverbs 18 NIV:
"Fools find no pleasure in understanding but delight in airing their own opinions." (vs 2)

"To answer before listening— that is folly and shame." (vs 13)

"The heart of the discerning acquires knowledge, for the ears of the wise seek it out." (vs 15)

Solomon writes about Speaking and Listening - two activities that most people engage in on a daily or hourly basis - sometimes more often. Here's a popular saying that makes a lot of sense: "God gave us two ears but only one mouth." The idea is that we should listen twice as much as we speak.

There are two types of people mentioned in these verses as well: Foolish people - who engage their mouths quickly and often; and Wise people - who use their ears as a first response and gain knowledge. So, practice "gathering" information by listening before "giving" opinionated oration.

122. PROPER PERSPECTIVE
"Not to us, Lord, not to us but to your name be the glory, because of your love and faithfulness."   Psalm 115:1 NIV

Many people want to take the credit for their own success and accomplishments. Some even crave recognition for their great ideas and suggestions. The psalmist reminds us to keep all things in proper perspective. Where do we get our life from? Where do we get our talents and imagination from? There are no "self-made" people.

We are all the result of our Creator, the Lord our God. All we are and all we have are a direct result of His creative design, His unmerited love, and His faithfulness to us. So, it's not to us that any glory belongs - ALL THE GLORY belongs to the Lord. Never try to steal any of it for yourself. Be sure to humble yourself and give Him proper recognition.

123. NO SUCH LUCK
"The Lord protects the unwary; when I was brought low, he saved me." Psalm 116:6 NIV

Have you ever observed something happening right before your eyes and asked yourself, "What just happened?" Maybe an accident just occurred right in front of you, but you were not affected. Or possibly you were made aware of some danger that was nearby, but you had no clue.

There are times when we are careless or not paying attention, or when we were oblivious to what was happening around us, or that we are miraculously preserved from danger. THAT WAS GOD'S PROTECTION OR INTERVENTION. If we are "Believers in Christ" then there is no such thing as "luck" or "chance". The Lord is our Protector.

124. PURSUE WITH A PURPOSE
"Whoever pursues righteousness and love finds life, prosperity and honor." Proverbs 21:21 NIV

The active word in this verse is "Pursues", which means much more than just going after something or giving an attempt. To pursue means to follow in order to overtake or capture; to chase, to strive to gain; to seek to attain or accomplish.

This verse mentions that which is to be sought after - and it's not life, prosperity, and honor. No, those are the result of following after righteousness and love. Don't confuse or mix up the "target" with the "rewards". Aim and fire at the "bullseye" in order to win the prize. If you miss the true "bullseye" you will miss the true prize.

125. GOD IS TRUE TO HIS WORD

"Praise the Lord, all you nations; extol him, all you peoples. For great is his love toward us, and the faithfulness of the Lord endures forever. Praise the Lord."   Psalm 117:1-2 NIV

Faithfulness - we usually associate this word with "being dependable". Other words that can be connected to this word are stability, integrity, and reliability. In addition, in the Old Testament, this word is the principle Hebrew word used to signify "truth".

Because God loves His people, He can be forever trusted to be TRUE TO HIS WORD. We can depend on what He has said about Himself - He will never leave us or forsake us, we can cast all our cares on Him because He cares for us, He will provide for us and protect us, He will comfort us, etc., etc.

Do you trust in His faithfulness?

126. OPEN OUR EYES TO SEE

"Open my eyes that I may see wonderful things in your law."
Psalm 119:18 NIV

Why do so many people shy away from reading the Word of God - the Bible? There are a few thoughts on this. One is that it is too hard to understand for "common" people - that only the most "religious", or only theologians can understand it. And there's the idea that the Bible is outdated for today's culture - or not relevant for today. Here's another excuse - "I don't have time".

The psalmist had the correct attitude regarding the Word, or law, of God. He revealed that his understanding was limited and that he needed help in seeing clearly. It appears that he was aware that there were "wonderful" things contained in God's law. His response? He asked for his eyes (understanding) to be opened. This is the key to unlocking the wonderful things contained in God's Word. The Bible contains Spiritually inspired writings, so we must pray for Spiritual revelation to see clearly.

127. COMFORT IN SUFFERING COMES FROM CONFIDENCE
"My comfort in my suffering is this: Your promise preserves my life."
Psalm 119:50 NIV

Suffering is a part of life. I don't know anyone who has not suffered at some time and in some way. Suffering has different levels for different people, and it is handled differently by those affected by it. The question is, how do you react when suffering comes your way?

This Psalmist gives his personal solution for obtaining relief from his own suffering - he knew and trusted in God's promises to preserve his life. His confidence in God brought him comfort. Though suffering may be inevitable, our comfort and preservation comes from the confidence we place in the Lord's promises.

128. A GOOD FRIEND SMELLS GOOD
"Perfume and incense bring joy to the heart, and the pleasantness of a friend springs from their heartfelt advice."   Proverbs 27:9 NIV

Friends - everyone needs friends. God, in creation, even said that it was not good for man to be alone, so He made a "helper" for him. We realize that this helper for Adam was a woman - Eve - and that Eve was much more than a "friend". However, the concept of companionship is seen in Proverbs 27:9 as well as in creation.

The author of this Proverb compares the pleasantness of a friend with the aroma of perfume. A good perfume, especially the expensive ones, can stimulate our sense of smell to the point of attraction or excitement. Having a good friend close by, who can offer heartfelt advice, and vice versa, is more valuable to us than the most expensive perfume or cologne. Do you have good friends that have a "good aroma"?

129. AFFLICTION'S BENEFITS
"It was good for me to be afflicted so that I might learn your decrees." Psalm 119:71 NIV

Take a look at the definition of the word <u>affliction</u>: "A state of pain, distress, or grief; misery; a cause of mental or bodily pain, as sickness, loss, calamity, or persecution".

How then could anyone, let alone this psalmist, say that being afflicted is a good thing? Well, have you ever heard a saying found in some gyms: "No Pain - No Gain"? So, there is some truth to the benefit of pain and suffering. For those who work out in the gym, the benefits are increased endurance, increased strength, and toned muscles.

The psalmist identifies another benefit from affliction - by enduring various afflictions he might better learn God's decrees (God's laws and His order). If you are open to this, you can learn more about the value of obeying the Lord in the middle of difficult circumstances.

130. BE CAREFUL OF THE COMPANY YOU KEEP
"Away from me, you evildoers, that I may keep the commands of my God!" Psalm 119:115 NIV

From what the Psalmist writes here it appears that he knows the danger of associating with those who are evil.

I found an anonymous quote that sheds some light on this thought: "It Is better to be alone, than in the wrong company. Tell me who your best friends are, and I will tell you who you are. If you run with wolves, you will learn how to howl. But, if you associate with eagles, you will learn how to soar to great heights."

It's great to have some non-Christian friends, but we should be good examples of Christ in front of them so they can see Jesus in us. Our hope is that they would be drawn to Christ. We need to be careful though, that friends don't negatively influence us and we find ourselves being drawn away from our God and Savior.

131. PERFECTION IN EVERY WORD
""Every word of God is flawless; he is a shield to those who take refuge in him. Do not add to his words, or he will rebuke you and prove you a liar." Proverbs 30:5-6 NIV

Isn't it interesting that there are so many books available to be read? There are books of fiction, books of facts, books of history, books about science, and books about every subject under the sun. But there is only one book that stands out above them all - the Bible, the Word of God (the number-one best seller of all time).

The Bible itself tells us in Proverbs 30, that every word of God is true and accurate - flawless. That means there are no mistakes, contrary to what many people believe. The words of God, from God to man, are not from a human source. Therefore, we must have a spiritual connection, or relationship, with God in order to understand and believe His words. We cannot, we must not, add to, or give our own human interpretations to what God has said. Sincerely seek for understanding of the Truth. Be very careful when you say, "God says . . ."

132. OUR SOURCE OF HELP
"I lift up my eyes to the mountains— where does my help come from? My help comes from the Lord, the Maker of heaven and earth."
Psalm 121:1-2 NIV

It is often said that men refuse to ask for directions when they are lost. It may be an "ego thing". What is it about not wanting help? If we are honest with ourselves, we would realize that we all need the assistance of another person at times.

The writer of this Psalm is rhetorically asking a question about the source of his help. There was no hesitation in his answer for obvious reasons. One, he knew he needed help, and two, he knew his Helper - not just anyone, it was the Creator Himself.

Let us never think that we can "go it alone"! So, let's humble ourselves and look to the Lord for help.

133. ANTICIPATION AND EXPECTATION
"I lift up my eyes to you, to you who sit enthroned in heaven. As the eyes of slaves look to the hand of their master, as the eyes of a female slave look to the hand of her mistress, so our eyes look to the Lord our God, till he shows us his mercy." Psalm 123:1-2 NIV

As I read this Psalm this morning, I thought of our dogs - and some of you may be able to relate to this if you have dogs. It seems like whenever we sit down to eat something they are constantly at our feet, looking up at us with their sad eyes, begging for food, as if they are starving.

Have you ever pictured yourself looking up to the Lord that way? The psalmist sure did. And notice how he said, "till He shows us His mercy". This is how we should wait on the Lord when we are in need. But we don't have to beg, or whine, looking up with sad "puppy dog eyes" - just look up to the Lord with anticipation and expectation. HE WILL SHOW US MERCY AND ANSWER OUR REQUESTS.

134. STRAIGHT PATHS AND LESS HAZARDS

"Listen, my son, accept what I say, and the years of your life will be many. I instruct you in the way of wisdom and lead you along straight paths. When you walk, your steps will not be hampered; when you run, you will not stumble."   Proverbs 4:10-12 NIV

I really like going to Maui. There are some great places to hike. One of them is the Nakalele Blowhole on the windward side (East) of the Island. The view from the road is awesome, but the hike down the cliff to the Blowhole is even more enjoyable and breath-taking. However, there are sharp rocks and steep areas to navigate through, along with the wet slippery rocks below. This makes the venture somewhat hazardous.

That hike came to mind when I read this Proverb. By following God's Wisdom and adhering to it, life's paths are made straight and the sharp slippery rocks will not trip us up. Thus, Wisdom makes the hazards of life more avoidable. Use Wisdom and follow the Lord.

135. EFFORTS FOR THE KINGDOM ARE NOT IN VAIN

"Those who sow with tears will reap with songs of joy. Those who go out weeping, carrying seed to sow, will return with songs of joy, carrying sheaves with them." Psalm 126:5-6 NIV

Notice in these verses that sowing seed is associated with tears and weeping. Whatever it is that you exert your energy toward, there seems to be an element of pain and suffering that goes along with it. Maybe it's not excruciating pain that is felt, but there may be a pain from weariness.

However, notice also the reward that comes as a result of such laboring. Songs of Joy are associated with the product or reward that results from the intense effort that is put forth.

So, take joy in knowing that your efforts in serving God, praying for family and friends, using your talents and skills and resources for the Kingdom of God are not in vain.

136. JUST DO IT!

"Go to the ant, you sluggard; consider its ways and be wise! It has no commander, no overseer or ruler, yet it stores its provisions in summer and gathers its food at harvest." Proverbs 6:6-8 NIV

You have probably heard of the story about "The Turtle and the Hare". Haven't you? Well, this Proverb speaks about an ant and a sluggard. A sluggard is a person who is habitually inactive or lazy. Do you know anyone like that? Solomon writes about the contrasting difference between the small ant and a lazy person.

What I like about the characteristics of the ant is that it works hard and pursues survival. It has no instruction manual, but instinctively does what is necessary. Solomon wisely gives instruction to those who may be lazy and unproductive: "Consider its ways". In other words, watch how the ant works hard, purposefully, without being told what to do, and imitate its actions. Therefore, don't procrastinate, see what needs to be done and just do it!

137. SOWING AND REAPING

"Blessed are all who fear the Lord, who walk in obedience to him. You will eat the fruit of your labor; blessings and prosperity will be yours."
Psalm 128:1-2 NIV

Most of us are familiar with the saying, "You Reap what You Sow." Galatians 6:7 says this as well. In fact, this principle is found throughout the Bible. And, planting seeds (sowing) in a garden is something we should all try at some point in time - if we haven't already done so. This is a rare experience for many people these days because of all the grocery stores, markets, and CostCo stores. Just pick up what you need - you don't have to wait.

Life is full of "sowing seeds and reaping a harvest". Today's reading in Psalm 128 mentions two kinds of "seeds" that can be sown: the fear of the Lord and walking in obedience. These "seeds" will always produce a crop - not natural food (fruits and vegetables), but Blessings and Prosperity. The principal of sowing and reaping never fails. What seeds will you be sowing today - seeds of anger and rebellion, or seeds of obedience to the Lord?

138. NO RECORD OF WRONGS

"If you, Lord, kept a record of sins, Lord, who could stand? But with you there is forgiveness, so that we can, with reverence, serve you."
Psalm 130:3-4 NIV

How many of your sins do you remember? How many times have others sinned against you, and you have kept a mental record of them? It's not so much that "forgetting" sin is the focus here, but the "keeping of a record" of those sins. We are instructed to FORGIVE - but sometimes we can't FORGET because it is etched in our memory banks.

The Lord, however, has not kept a record of our sins. None of us could ever feel comfortable around Him if we knew He was "hanging our sins and mistakes over our head", to maybe bring them up again and throw them in our face. How, or why, would we serve Him or give Him the reverence He deserves if He did that to us? So, don't do that to others. *"Love keeps no records of wrongs"* (1 Corinthians 13:5), but we must recognize our sins, confess them to Jesus, and then walk in freedom.

139. IS YOUR FRUIT GIVING LIFE TO OTHERS?
"The fruit of the righteous is a tree of life, and the one who is wise saves lives." Proverbs 11:30 NIV

The person who lives a good, righteous, and fruitful life has a positive effect on those they associate with. This Proverb states that they are like a tree of life to them, encouraging their souls and setting a good example to follow. The very life we live in the presence of others can hopefully save them from a life of destruction.

Therefore, think of your own life (how you act or react, how you speak, how you care, etc.) - this is your "fruit". Is the "fruit" of your tree nourishing others, giving them life, or is your fruit withered or rotten? Strive to be like the person in Psalm 1, who always produces fruit "in season". *You will need to read all of Psalm 1 to see how that is accomplished.

140. NEGATIVE AND POSITIVE POWER OF WORDS

"The words of the reckless pierce like swords, but the tongue of the wise brings healing."   Proverbs 12:18 NIV

"Anxiety weighs down the heart, but a kind word cheers it up."
Proverbs 12:25 NIV

WORDS - we all use them. We either give them or receive them, and in a variety of ways. There are written words, digital words, verbal and nonverbal words. Using words recklessly can cause hurt and anxiety. However, using words cautiously and wisely can bring comfort and healing.

Words are like knives or scalpels. They are sharp and can cut deep - either for harm (as in a fight) or for surgical procedures to promote a cure for healing. So, take great care before you use your words. Ask yourself if you are a destroyer or a doctor; a scoundrel or a surgeon.

141. HOW TO HANDLE AUTHORITY

"Whoever scorns instruction will pay for it, but whoever respects a command is rewarded."   Proverbs 13:13 NIV

How do you handle, or receive, instructions from a superior (a boss, a teacher, a coach, a police officer, etc.)? It's not that these individuals are any better than you - but they have positions of authority along with a greater responsibility for getting tasks done through the people they oversee.

There are two ways identified in this Proverb regarding a response to instructions or commands - either scorning or respecting. There is a great reward in responding properly when given directions. The best way to insure we respond correctly is to recognize the authority in that one giving the instructions or commands. God has set up "Authority" on the earth in order to maintain order. Rejecting this principle of authority is rejecting God.

142. PRAISE THAT NEVER ENDS
"Give thanks to the Lord, for He is good. His love endures forever."
Psalm 136:1 NIV

Psalm 136 is sometimes referred to as "The Great Hallel" (Praise). There is a phrase repeated 26 times throughout the entire Psalm: "His love endures forever".

Many years ago, there was a popular children's song that appeared in the album "Lamb Chop's Sing-Along, Play-Along" by puppeteer Shari Lewis. It is called "The Song That Never Ends". Its verses were repeated over and over and over again until people either became weary of singing or extremely annoyed. Children like things like that, but adults . . . not so much.

My prayer is that we will always give thanks to the Lord because of His great Love, and that we would never get tired of telling Him. It's like a "Praise that Never Ends" to our God who's Love Endures forever!

143. EARLY WARNING SYSTEM
"Pride goes before destruction, a haughty spirit before a fall."
Proverbs 16:18 NIV

There is a lot of attention today regarding Early Warning Systems, especially when it comes to earthquakes, tsunamis, nuclear attacks, disease outbreaks, hurricanes, etc. These systems can enable people to prepare for the impending danger and act accordingly to hopefully save lives.

Proverbs 16:18 is a Biblical Early Warning System. In order to hopefully prevent a person from "falling" and suffering destruction, there is an obvious "Warning Sign" - that sign is PRIDE, a haughty spirit. Let's examine ourselves and pay attention to the warning signs, then we can make the changes to avoid destruction.

144. WHAT DOES GOD THINK OF YOU?
"How precious to me are your thoughts, God! How vast is the sum of them! Were I to count them, they would outnumber the grains of sand— when I awake, I am still with you." Psalm 139:17-18 NIV

A part of our human nature - our makeup - is to consider what others think of us. Many people, before leaving their homes, want to try and look their best. They shower, brush their teeth, comb their hair, and dress themselves with clean and neat (and matching) clothes. Why? Because they want to look "presentable" to others. I know, and you know, that not everyone is like that.

Some people even fear what others think of them, so they try desperately to please everyone. David wrote in this Psalm about the Lord's thoughts toward him, and how he valued or cherished them. David also added that the Lord's thoughts were vast or countless.

Instead of being overly concerned or worried about what others think of us, let us consider, and dwell on, what the Lord thinks of us. Are we "presentable" to Him?

145. THE WISE LISTEN AND PAY ATTENTION
"Listen to advice and accept discipline, and at the end you will be counted among the wise." Proverbs 19:20 NIV

Do you know what it feels like to be included in the top 10% of the people around you? Maybe you have been in some kind of competition and you "made the cut", versus being eliminated or sent home. Or, maybe you were the one who didn't get picked and know what that feels like.

To be "counted among the wise" would be a great honor. The author of most of the Proverbs, including the one we are reading today, was called "the wisest person of all time". How would one become included in this arena? By listening to good advice (Godly counsel) and by willingly receiving discipline or correction, you will be given a seat with the wise. Listen, Trust, and Obey.

146. INCENSE AND SACRIFICE
"I call to you, Lord, come quickly to me; hear me when I call to you. May my prayer be set before you like incense; may the lifting up of my hands be like the evening sacrifice."   Psalm 141:1-2 NIV

Close your eyes and get a mental picture of your prayers flowing from your lips and rising toward heaven as smoke from burning incense. Imagine the fragrant aroma permeating the atmosphere. Meditate on this for a while. This is the picture David was trying to paint as he wrote about calling on the Lord. I can almost imagine the Lord inhaling deeply, filling His nostrils with our prayers.

Also, picture in your mind raising your hands toward the Lord in heaven, offering yourself as a "sacrifice" to Him. Imagine a burnt offering on the altar, totally consumed with nothing else to burn. Then ask yourself: "Am I Giving my all to the Lord?"

IMAGINE - it's easy if you try.

147.   IS YOUR HEART LIKE A VACANT LOT?
"Haughty eyes and a proud heart— the unplowed field of the wicked—
produce sin."   Proverbs 21:4 NIV

A vacant lot is a real "eyesore". There is one in our neighborhood near
a main street. Weeds, trash, dried grass, rocks, and broken glass can
be easily seen. Someone has neglected this piece of land. And this is
how Solomon describes a person with a proud spirit - "the unplowed
field of the wicked".

What this Proverb implies is that haughty, proud, conceited people
really have a heart like a vacant lot - unplowed, abandoned, and
neglected. The only product of such a heart is trash and weeds - or sin.
So, examine your heart (your mind and desires). Turn up the soil of
your heart. If you find anything harmful, useless or ungodly, humble
yourself and get rid of those things. Then, it will be prepared to receive
"good seed" and produce a crop of goodness and righteousness. The
labor is well worth the reward.

148.   WHAT'S IN IT FOR ME?
"Humility is the fear of the Lord; its wages are riches and honor and
life."   Proverbs 22:4 NIV

Many questions came to mind as I focused on this verse: "Does it pay
to be good?" "Does it pay to be honest?" "Does it pay to be humble?"

Also, in Matthew 19, Jesus was telling the disciples how hard it was for
a rich man to enter the kingdom of God. And, Peter spoke up and
asked, *"We have left everything to follow you! What then will there be*
for us?"   Matthew 19:27 NIV

It seems like everyone wants to know "WHAT'S IN IT FOR ME?"

Well, Proverbs 22:4 gives a great answer with a great reward. Fearing the Lord and being humble brings "wages" to those who live this way - the wages paid are riches and honor and life. That's what is in it for us!

149. WHY DOES GOD CARE FOR US?
"Lord, what are human beings that you care for them, mere mortals that you think of them?" Psalm 144:3 NIV

There are things that just don't mix together: light and darkness; oil and water; sweet and sour; right and wrong. And David, in this Psalm, mentions the Lord God and humans. We know God is spirit and eternal, and we are flesh and mortal. The definition of "mortal" is: belonging to this world, subject to death". So, why would God care for us who are so different - so opposite from Him? Why would He create something so different from Himself?

I can't really comprehend all the reasons that God cares for us mortals. However, in His Word (the Bible) we are told that "God SO LOVED the world", and while we were His enemies/sinners, He (Jesus) died for us. It appears, to me, that God destroys opposites, or opposition, by His Great Love in order to make us "one with Him" and to give us life. The best way to destroy an enemy is to make them your friend.

150. GOD'S HELPING HAND
"The Lord upholds all who fall and lifts up all who are bowed down." Psalm 145:14 NIV

There's an old saying that reminds me of this verse: "Never kick a man when he's down." When we stumble and fall, we are in a position of vulnerability. Sometimes it's obvious to all, but other times it's in secret. When we are down, we don't need any harsh criticism or speculation. We need a helping hand - from others, and especially from God.

If God's arms are always there to hold us up, shouldn't we do the same for others? Let's not be quick to judge or criticize someone who is struggling against sin, guilt, or depression. Lift that person up in prayer and encourage them. Some day you may need a helping hand too. Will you find it?

FINAL WORDS

It is my prayer that you will develop a healthy daily habit of reading God's precious Word. The more you read, meditate, and memorize the Scriptures, the healthier your spirit becomes. We spend so much time feeding the "natural man", it's no wonder we struggle with our flesh at times. Many years ago, a friend of mine recommended that I read a certain book. That book challenged me to start a habit of reading daily. In the past, I had never really enjoyed reading. Now, I can't stop. So, I hope this book will also challenge you to read on a consistent basis. Let the Lord speak to your spirit as you read. This is what I have tried to do in this book and in my first book, *"24 Karat" Daily Nuggets of Inspiration.* I hope you will enjoy the short messages and, who knows, you just might be inspired to do the same thing and start sharing them with your circle of friends and family. May God Bless you.

Pastor John Weigelt
New Life Christian Center, Inc.

Made in the USA
Monee, IL
05 December 2021

83898859R00059